C304 019 573 649 48

771

KEYWORTH		17. MAY 07.
K2/04	28 FEB 2005	31. AUG 07.
04. MAR 04		
16. MAR 04.	22 DEC 2005	03. JUL 08
		28. FEB 09.
22. MAR 04.	GOTHAM	
01. 05. 04.		17. SEP 09.
13 MAY 2004	KEYWORTH 2/07	
	17. MAY 08	30. JAN 10.
30. JUL 04		23. FEB 10.
EAST LEAKE		
09. OCT 04		21. DEC 10.
SUTTON BONINGTON		19. MAR 11
		JUN 12

ANDREW, M.
Nottinghamshire

COUNTY LIBRARY

Nottinghamshire County Council
Community Services

Please return / renew by the
last date shown.

Francis Frith's

NOTTINGHAMSHIRE
LIVING MEMORIES

MARTIN ANDREW is an architectural and landscape historian and writer on outdoor matters, and the Conservation Officer for Wycombe District Council in Buckinghamshire. He specialises in the landscape of lowland England, and combines his love of history, landscape and architecture in his writing. Since 1978 he has lived in Haddenham in Buckinghamshire with his wife and children; he is a keen long-distance walker, and enjoys riding his classic motor cycle round the country lanes of the Chilterns. He was born in Doncaster, but spent most of his childhood in Ealing and Carshalton in Surrey. After university he worked for the Greater London Council's Historic Buildings Division, Buckinghamshire County Council and Salisbury District Council before joining Wycombe District Council in 1990.

NOTTINGHAMSHIRE

LIVING MEMORIES

MARTIN ANDREW

First published in the United Kingdom in 2003 by
Frith Book Company Ltd

Hardback Edition 2003
ISBN 1-85937-668-1

British Library Cataloguing in Publication Data

Nottinghamshire Living Memories
Martin Andrew

Frith Book Company Ltd
Frith's Barn, Teffont,
Salisbury, Wiltshire SP3 5QP
Tel: +44 (0) 1722 716 376
Email: info@francisfrith.co.uk
www.francisfrith.co.uk

Printed and bound in Great Britain

Front Cover: **NOTTINGHAM,** *Old Market Square and the
Council House c1955* N50046
Frontispiece: **BURTON JOYCE,** *The Poplar Walk c1965*
B606015

*The colour-tinting is for illustrative purposes only, and is not intended to be
historically accurate*

AS WITH ANY HISTORICAL DATABASE THE FRITH ARCHIVE IS CONSTANTLY
BEING CORRECTED AND IMPROVED, AND THE PUBLISHERS WOULD
WELCOME INFORMATION ON OMISSIONS OR INACCURACIES

CONTENTS

FRANCIS FRITH
VICTORIAN PIONEER

FRANCIS FRITH, founder of the world-famous photographic archive, was a complex and multi-talented man. A devout Quaker and a highly successful Victorian businessman, he was philosophic by nature and pioneering in outlook.

By 1855 he had already established a wholesale grocery business in Liverpool, and sold it for the astonishing sum of £200,000, which is the equivalent today of over £15,000,000. Now a very rich man, he was able to indulge his passion for travel. As a child he had pored over travel books written by early explorers, and his fancy and imagination had been stirred by family holidays to the sublime mountain regions of Wales and Scotland. 'What lands of spirit-stirring and enriching scenes and places!' he had written. He was to return to these scenes of grandeur in later years to 'recapture the thousands of vivid and tender memories', but with a different purpose. Now in his thirties, and captivated by the new science of photography, Frith set out on a series of pioneering journeys up the Nile and to the Near East that occupied him from 1856 unti 1860.

INTRIGUE AND EXPLORATION

These far-flung journeys were packed with intrigue and adventure. In his life story, written when he was sixty-three, Frith tells of being held captive by bandits, and of fighting 'an awful midnight battle to the very point of surrender with a deadly pack of hungry, wild dogs'. Wearing flowing Arab costume, Frith arrived at Akaba by camel seventy years before Lawrence of Arabia, where he encountered 'desert princes and rival sheikhs, blazing with jewel-hilted swords'.

He was the first photographer to venture beyond the sixth cataract of the Nile. Africa was still the mysterious 'Dark Continent', and Stanley and Livingstone's historic meeting was a decade into the future. The conditions for picture taking confound belief. He laboured for hours in his wicker dark-room in the sweltering heat of the desert, while the volatile chemicals fizzed dangerously in their trays. Back in London he exhibited his photographs and was 'rapturously cheered' by members of the Royal Society. His reputation as a photographer was made overnight.

VENTURE OF A LIFE-TIME

Characteristically, Frith quickly spotted the opportunity to create a new business as a specialist publisher of photographs. He lived in an era of immense and sometimes violent change. For the poor in the early part of Victoria's reign work was exhausting and the hours long, and people had precious little free time to enjoy themselves. Most people had no transport other than a cart or gig at their disposal, and rarely

business one only has to look at the catalogue issued by Frith & Co in 1886: it runs to some 670 pages, listing not only many thousands of views of the British Isles but also many photographs of most European countries, and China, Japan, the USA and Canada - note the sample page shown here from the hand-written Frith & Co ledgers recording the pictures. By 1890 Frith had created the greatest specialist photographic publishing company in the world, with over 2,000 sales outlets - more than the combined number that Boots and WH Smith have today! The picture on the next page shows the Frith & Co display board at Ingleton in the Yorkshire Dales (left of window). Beautifully constructed with a mahogany frame and gilt inserts, it could display up to a dozen local scenes.

POSTCARD BONANZA

The ever-popular holiday postcard we know today took many years to develop. In 1870 the Post Office issued the first plain cards, with a pre-printed stamp on one face. In 1894 they allowed other publishers' cards to be sent through the mail with an attached adhesive halfpenny stamp. Demand grew rapidly, and in 1895 a new size of postcard was permitted called the court card, but there was little room for illustration. In 1899, a year after Frith's death, a new card measuring 5.5 x 3.5 inches became the standard format, but it was not until 1902 that the divided back came into being, so that the address and message could be on one face and a full-size illustration on the other. Frith & Co were in the vanguard of postcard development: Frith's sons Eustace and Cyril continued their father's monumental task, expanding the number of views offered to the public and recording more and more places in Britain, as the coasts and countryside were opened up to mass travel.

Francis Frith had died in 1898 at his villa in Cannes, his great project still growing. The archive he created continued in business for another seventy years. By 1970 it contained over a third of a million pictures showing 7,000 British towns and villages.

travelled far beyond the boundaries of their own town or village. However, by the 1870s the railways had threaded their way across the country, and Bank Holidays and half-day Saturdays had been made obligatory by Act of Parliament. All of a sudden the working man and his family were able to enjoy days out and see a little more of the world.

With typical business acumen, Francis Frith foresaw that these new tourists would enjoy having souvenirs to commemorate their days out. In 1860 he married Mary Ann Rosling and set out on a new career: his aim was to photograph every city, town and village in Britain. For the next thirty years he travelled the country by train and by pony and trap, producing fine photographs of seaside resorts and beauty spots that were keenly bought by millions of Victorians. These prints were painstakingly pasted into family albums and pored over during the dark nights of winter, rekindling precious memories of summer excursions.

THE RISE OF FRITH & CO

Frith's studio was soon supplying retail shops all over the country. To meet the demand he gathered about him a small team of photographers, and published the work of independent artist-photographers of the calibre of Roger Fenton and Francis Bedford. In order to gain some understanding of the scale of Frith's

FRANCIS FRITH'S LEGACY

Frith's legacy to us today is of immense significance and value, for the magnificent archive of evocative photographs he created provides a unique record of change in the cities, towns and villages throughout Britain over a century and more. Frith and his fellow studio photographers revisited locations many times down the years to update their views, compiling for us an enthralling and colourful pageant of British life and character.

We are fortunate that Frith was dedicated to recording the minutiae of everyday life. For it is this sheer wealth of visual data, the painstaking chronicle of changes in dress, transport, street layouts, buildings, housing, engineering and landscape that captivates us so much today. His remarkable images offer us a powerful link with the past and with the lives of our ancestors.

THE VALUE OF THE ARCHIVE TODAY

Computers have now made it possible for Frith's many thousands of images to be accessed almost instantly. Frith's images are increasingly used as visual resources, by social historians, by researchers into genealogy and ancestry, by architects and town planners, and by teachers involved in local history projects.

In addition, the archive offers every one of us an opportunity to examine the places where we and our families have lived and worked down the years. Highly successful in Frith's own era, the archive is now, a century and more on, entering a new phase of popularity. Historians consider the Francis Frith Collection to be of prime national importance. It is the only archive of its kind remaining in private ownership. Francis Frith's archive is now housed in an historic timber barn in the beautiful village of Teffont in Wiltshire. Its founder would not recognize the archive office as it is today. In place of the many thousands of dusty boxes containing glass plate negatives and an all-pervading odour of photographic chemicals, there are now ranks of computer screens. He would be amazed to watch his images travelling round the world at unimaginable speeds through internet lines.

The archive's future is both bright and exciting. Francis Frith, with his unshakeable belief in making photographs available to the greatest number of people, would undoubtedly approve of what is being done today with his lifetime's work. His photographs depicting our shared past are now bringing pleasure and enlightenment to millions around the world a century and more after his death.

NOTTINGHAMSHIRE
AN INTRODUCTION

Nottinghamshire is a county steeped in history, and it likes to remind you every time you enter it by road that it is 'Robin Hood Country'. This rather undersells the rest of Nottinghamshire, but Robin Hood is obviously important to the tourist industry, and the 100,000 acres of Sherwood Forest do represent about a fifth of the county's size. Robin Hood, of course, probably did not exist; and if he did, Yorkshire is the earlier location for the tales. Nottinghamshire became the location for the stories later in the Middle Ages, with various real places and people added: Sherwood Forest where the Merry Men lived, Edwinstowe where Robin married Maid Marian, and of course the Sheriff of Nottingham and Nottingham Castle. Nottinghamshire nowadays trades on all this with a Robin Hood Festival in Sherwood Forest, the Robin Hood Pageant at Nottingham Castle (where a superb statue reminds visitors of him in the unlikely event of them forgetting), the Tales of

MANSFIELD, *c1955* M184066

Robin Hood Experience in Nottingham, and the World of Robin Hood near Ollerton, as well as the Robin Hood Way long-distance footpath.

This book is intended to give a portrait of Nottinghamshire within living memory, with the views mostly taken in the 1950s and 1960s, and a few from the 1940s. This was a time when the coal mines still functioned all along the west of the county, and when huge coal-fired power stations were built along the River Trent and were supplied by barge and railway. This was a time (before Beeching's drastic cuts) when branch railway lines could take you to virtually every village, and when Gresley's great steam locomotives hauled the Flying Scotsman and other expresses along the east coast main line of the London and North Eastern Region (LNER) of the nationalised railway network; they passed through Newark and Retford on their way to Doncaster and the north. This was a time when the main roads like the A1 (the Great North Road) choked the centres of un-bypassed towns and villages, and when the once important canals faded into neglect.

Viewing these photographs, we can occasionally see the first signs of the great phase of revival through rebuilding that convinced planners, architects, councils and developers that rebuilding was the only way of pulling moribund towns out of the doldrums of the 1950s. This, of course, adds to the value of the Frith collection's 1950s and 1960s archive photographs of a world just about to be lost. Despite these images, which could so easily make this book a catalogue of buildings lost and opportunities missed or bungled, a great deal survived to keep Nottinghamshire's towns recognisable and to provide continuity with the past - so valuable in giving people a sense of place and identity.

A brief look at what the city of Nottingham itself lost or misplaced gives a flavour of the mid-20th century's approach to these matters. In many cases, only single buildings were demolished, such as the Black Boy Hotel in Long Row (N50046, page 15) or the Turkish Baths in Upper Parliament Street (N50064, page 19). However, there were grander schemes such as Maid Marian Way, which was intended as the first part of an inner ring road, but was stalled in the utterly justified face of great objections. The west part was built between 1958 and 1966, and destroyed numerous old buildings in a wide swathe between Collin Street and Derby Road. The space left over on each side was filled by office blocks, mostly glass and steel-framed, which utterly ruin the view eastwards from the castle. The 1960s major shopping malls of Broad Marsh and the Victoria Centre took no notice of the older street patterns beneath, and the Victoria Centre involved the 1967 demolition of all of the fine 1900 Victoria Station except for its clock tower.

One could go on. But there are pluses: the decline of the Lace Market quarter in this period kept it broadly intact for more enlightened times, and in the last decade or so the area has seen progressively more restoration and refurbishment of the existing buildings. The High Pavement area also remains largely intact. In the centre, around the Old Market Place and Upper Parliament Street, the predominantly Victorian city is still dominant despite the rebuilding, some of which was crass (like the 1967 Market Square House) or just deadly dull (like the Littlewoods that replaced the exuberant 1897 Black Boy Hotel).

In smaller towns the pattern has been repeated. For example, good Victorian buildings in Bridge Place, Worksop, were replaced by the bland

Co-operative House in the late 1950s (W278087, page 75), now itself replaced, and further down Bridge Street much went to make way for the appalling 1970s Priory Shopping Centre. The exception to this is Newark: although many of its industrial buildings like breweries and maltings were demolished, it kept its historic town centre remarkably intact during the redevelopment craze, so its heritage is nowadays a positive asset that draws in visitors. Nottingham, of course expanded greatly at this time, continuing the pre-World War II growth trend, absorbing Carlton, Gedling, Arnold, Bestwood Park, Broxtowe, Strelley, Beeston and many other settlements, although not all these were absorbed politically.

Some of the new estates, such as the tower blocks of Basford Flats built between 1961 and 1978, proved highly unsatisfactory both structurally and socially, and they were demolished in 1985 to be replaced by conventional housing.

Industry in Nottingham has also changed a lot: the 1950s triumvirate of Boots, Raleigh Cycles and John Player has since has given way to more diversity. A lot of the dirty industries have gone (even brewing, which was such an important part of the city's economy), to be replaced by cleaner industries, commerce, service industries and offices, such as the Inland Revenue's down by the canal. The biggest change for Nottinghamshire has been the closure in the 1980s of virtually all

NEWSTEAD ABBEY, *The Dukeries c1955* N29320

the coal mines along the west side of the county, including Babbington, Arnold and Clifton collieries in the environs of Nottingham, D H Lawrence's father's Brinsley Pit near Eastwood, and Costhorpe near Langold. Harworth Colliery and a few others still function, but their survival into the 1980s was sustained by the great coal-fired power stations built in the 1960s along the River Trent such as Ratcliffe-on-Soar, Cottam and West Burton. The Nottinghamshire mines initially came through relatively unscathed during the first wave of closures after the miners' strike during Margaret Thatcher's premiership, but they could not outface the conversion of the River Trent power stations to gas - the last conversion has just been completed (2003). Thus villages have been left with little work, and Nottinghamshire's industrial heritage has taken a severe pounding.

On a more cheerful note we return to Sherwood Forest. Here, the great former ducal estates that from the 18th century gave the area its nickname of the Dukeries, and the forest itself, have fared better, providing major tourism opportunities. The Sherwood Forest Country Park's 450 acres and its Visitor Centre has been a great success, while the Dukeries estates have each fared differently. Clumber is in the safe hands of the National Trust. Rufford, in a precarious state after World War II and partly demolished in the 1950s, is at the heart of the 150-acre Rufford Country Park, opened in 1969 by the County Council, with the abbey and house ruins a stabilised and repaired centrepiece. Thoresby, for years threatened by mining subsidence, is now a luxury country house hotel, with no need for the miniature railway and other attractions to keep the roofs repaired.

Welbeck Abbey, which was for some years part house and part army sixth form college, is now a private residence once again, occupied by a grandson of the seventh Duke of Portland. Lord Byron's Newstead Abbey was presented to the City of Nottingham in 1931 and is open to the public. Thus the citizens of Nottingham and the towns of Nottinghamshire and Derbyshire to the west have beautiful countryside and places to roam within easy reach. Away from Nottingham, the Dukeries, and the mining villages along the west side of the county, we find a rolling, hedged typical Midland landscape. The fields are mostly 18th-century enclosed ones with straight hedges. The land becomes steadily flatter to the east and north-east, and culminates in the fen country of the Misterton Carrs. Here in the far north drainage channels thread the landscape, and the occasional low hills have villages on them, such as Gringley-on-the-Hill or Misterton. The eastern parts of the county are served by markets towns such as East Retford, Worksop, and Bingham, and there are many still attractive villages such as East Markham, Sutton-on-Trent, and Carlton in Lindrick, as well as the cathedral town of Southwell.

Throughout the northern part of the county we will see the Chesterfield Canal - in Worksop, Retford, Misterton, and at its junction with the River Trent at West Stockwith, where a warehouse of 1789 survives. In Worksop, Pickford's Depository, an old warehouse, still survives. The Chesterfield Canal, surveyed by the great canal builder James Brindley, took six years to complete, and opened in 1777. Built to carry coal to the Trent, it was taken over by a railway company in 1846, but it declined; the collapse of the Norwood

Tunnel over the border in Yorkshire in 1908 effectively cut the canal in two. The canal ceased to be a trading route in the 20th century, and stretches were used for leisure. In 1961 enthusiasts formed the Chesterfield Canal Society, and the section through Nottinghamshire is now largely restored as a continuous route through the county with all the locks fully functional. However, it is almost solely used for pleasure.

In 1974, along with the rest of England, Nottinghamshire's numerous old boroughs and rural district councils were abolished. They were replaced by eight district councils as the principal second layer of local government, with the County Council responsible for education, social services, minerals and so on. The County Borough of Nottingham became one of the districts, but several proud chartered boroughs disappeared into the new district councils. Worksop and East Retford were subsumed into Bassetlaw, and Southwell and Newark into Newark and Sherwood District Council.

I have known Nottinghamshire since my childhood in the 1950s. Indeed, my grandfather was born and lived his childhood in Misterton in the far north-east of the county. Journeys from London terminated in East Retford on the east coast main line, where we were met and driven to Gainsborough, on the Lincolnshire bank of the Trent, where my grandfather then lived. Drives to Barnby Moor's Old Bell, Clumber Park or to West Stockwith were seen as treats during our stays with my grandparents as a boy, and since then I have walked and toured the county extensively. It is in my view an under-rated county which crams a lot into its 550,000 acres, and I hope this portrait of the county in the 1950s and 1960s is an enjoyable one that reinforces the affection of those who know it well and whets the appetite of those who do not.

BUDBY, *The Village c1955* B833021

NOTTINGHAM AND THE WESTERN TRENT VALLEY

NOTTINGHAM
Old Market Square and the Council House c1955 N50046

The first chapter starts, fittingly, with a portrait of the county town, the city of Nottingham, in the 1950s. We start in the heart of the city in Old Market Square. The 18th-century Exchange was demolished in 1926 and replaced by the present Council House, opened in 1929 by the then Prince of Wales. The porticoed and domed building has shopping arcades in its ground floor, Exchange Arcade. To its left the pyramidal tower belongs to the famous Black Boy Hotel on Long Row, demolished in 1963 and replaced by an utterly gutless Littlewoods store.

15

NOTTINGHAM
Old Market Square c1955
N50054

Frith's photographer was looking west away from the Council House, with Long Row on the right. Some of the buildings on the left were replaced by the ten-storey office block Market Square House of 1967, whose bland glazed facades dominate the left side of the market place. The tall stone building on the right with the heavy cornice is Debenhams store on the corner of Market Street. This was originally Griffin & Spalding's store, and built in the 1920s.

NOTTINGHAM, *Market Street c1955*   N50050

Market Street leads from Old Market Place behind the photographer to Upper Parliament Street, and is terminated by the Theatre Royal's 1865 stuccoed front with its six-columned portico. On the right are buildings incorporated into Debenhams. Market Street now has tramlines again, the old tramways having gone before World War II. The new trams are not yet running (2003), but will no doubt be as successful as the new ones in Manchester or Croydon. Note the trolley bus wires, which were removed in 1966.

NOTTINGHAM
Queen Street c1955 N50052

Further east along Long Row, Frith's photographer was looking along Queen Street towards Upper Parliament Street. The road behind him is now pedestrianised, as is much of the area around the Council House. The 1895 post office on the left, faced in red sandstone, is now shops with offices over. Beyond the bus, the tower belongs to the old Empire music hall, which closed in 1958. Demolished in 1969, it has been replaced by stylish modern extensions to the Theatre Royal, the Royal Concert Hall.

NOTTINGHAM, *Upper Parliament Street c1955* N50064

This end of Upper Parliament Street, with the Theatre Royal halfway along and out of sight on the left, has seen many changes since the 1950s. On the left, the old Turkish Baths (the 1890s building with the columns to the top floor) and the florid News Theatre beyond were demolished in 1962 to make way for an eight-storey office block. The tall building beyond survives as The Stage pub, while on the right the 1928 faience-fronted Home Brewed Ales pub, The Fox, also survives, but renamed Number Ten.

NOTTINGHAM
Upper Parliament Street
c1955 N50066

Built in 1865, the fine stuccoed portico of the Theatre Royal is now flanked by modern buildings set further back, making the theatre a thoroughly up-to-date complex. The corner building on the right is faced in white faience; it opened in 1921 as a 1600-seater cinema, the Elite, with several restaurants. Closed in 1977, it became a bingo and social club until 1989, and is now offices. The spire downhill is that of the former Methodist church, built in 1874, and now the X-Gen Club (what would Wesley think?)

▶ **NOTTINGHAM**
Chapel Bar c1955
N50062

Long Row leads westwards uphill into Chapel Bar, now truncated by the Maid Marian Way roundabout junction with Derby Road. Maid Marian Way, built between 1958 and 1966, was a disaster: its crass dual carriageway cut a swathe that separates the castle area from the rest of the city. It was also lined by gruesome 1960s office blocks that replaced older and better buildings. Back in Chapel Bar, none of the foreground buildings survived the 1970s, and have all been rebuilt. In the distance is South Parade and Old Market Square.

◀ **NOTTINGHAM**
The Flying Horse Hotel
c1955 N50092

We now move east to The Poultry, the street along the south side of the Council House. The Flying Horse inn is one of the city centre's oldest surviving buildings, and a link with its Tudor past. Plaster panels inform us that it was established in the year 1483, but it looks more 16th-century. It closed as a pub to re-open, fully restored, in 1987 as a shopping arcade, and the building to the left now has a large Pegasus sculpture attached to it.

▲ **NOTTINGHAM,** *Trent Bridge c1950* N50036

This brief tour ignores the Georgian houses of High Pavement, the castle and the famous Lace Market area to descend to the River Trent. Originally the town extended only as far as the River Leen, but during the 19th century it advanced south across The Meadows to the River Trent. This view looks towards the 1871 cast iron Trent Bridge from the Victoria Embankment, a view much changed today, with the awful West Bridgford Hotel of 1962 (now Rushcliffe Civic Centre) replacing the trees, and the 1990s grandstands of Nottingham Forest Football Club rising beyond.

◀ **NOTTINGHAM**
Trent Bridge and the River Trent c1950 N50079

The bridge was designed by the splendidly named Marriott Ogle Tarbotton, the Corporation Engineer, to succeed a medieval stone bridge, itself a successor to the first wooden one built in AD920. This busy scene looking along the river terrace steps on Victoria Embankment shows the 1860s Town Arms pub by the bridge, the gabled building with bay windows and white stucco dressings. It survives today, renamed The Aviary. The factories have long gone.

NOTTINGHAM
*Ye Olde Trip to Jerusalem
Inn 1949* N50041

Reputedly founded in 1189,
the famous Ye Olde Trip to
Jerusalem Inn claims to be
the oldest in England. The
present buildings are 17th-
century at the earliest, with
an 18th-century taller left
bay. It incorporates cellars
cut into the sandstone of
Castle Hill. Behind it now is
the Brewhouse Yard
Museum (of Nottingham
life), opened in 1977, and
the Angel Row Gallery, both
housed in a row of brick
houses of about 1680.

▼ **NOTTINGHAM,** *The University, Hugh Stewart Hall c1955*   N50074

Nottingham University started in the city in 1881 on South Sherwood Street. In the 1920s Jesse Boot, founder of Boots the chemists, gave land to the west of Lenton, and University College moved here out of the city centre. Nottingham University College achieved independent university status in 1948; by then it stood in a park expanded from its original 60 acres to nearer 180 acres. Hugh Stewart Hall off Lenton Hall Drive, named after the Principal of the university from 1929 to 1934, was built in 1937, and incorporates Lenton Hall of 1804 (not seen in this view).

▶ **NOTTINGHAM**
The University, The Trent and Portland Buildings c1960
N50096

The first building was what is now known as the Trent Building (left, with the tall tower), designed by Morley Horder; it was begun in 1922 and opened in 1928 by George V, who immediately ennobled the generous Jesse Boot as Lord Trent. The lake and parkland setting was planned from the start. The right-hand building, the Portland Building, is brand-new in this view, having been completed only in 1956. It is also in Portland limestone. Its name relates to the Dukes of Portland of Welbeck Abbey.

◀ **NOTTINGHAM**
Wollaton Hall
c1955 N50022

Designed by Robert Smythson for Sir Francis Willoughby, who had made his fortune from coal, Wollaton Hall was built in the 1580s. It was sold by the 10th Lord Middleton, still a Willoughby, to the City of Nottingham in 1924. The 500 acres of deer park was incorporated in the city boundaries in 1932, but only the east side, a strip along the north side, and a strip along the west side were developed for housing; the city retained a goodly chunk, and maintained the building and grounds well.

▶ **STAPLEFORD**
The Roach c1955 S718006

The second section of this chapter starts to the west of the city in Stapleford, close to the Derbyshire border, which follows the River Erewash southwards to the River Trent. Stapleford, now virtually a satellite of Nottingham, grew up from a village of lace factories and framework knitters' houses. Its character is now that of a Victorian industrial town, as this view shows; we are at the main crossroads in the town centre, with Church Street off to the right. The corner shops are now a Nottingham Building Society branch.

STAPLEFORD
Derby Road c1955 S718009

This view looks back north-east towards the start of Nottingham Road and the crossroads we saw in view S718006 (on page 27). Most of the buildings and shops in this view survive today, except for the Nonconformist church, which was demolished in the 1980s and replaced by shops. The white building in the distance is The Chequers Inn at the start of Nottingham Road. To the right are the front gardens of 1880s semi-detached houses.

STAPLEFORD, *The Church c1955* S718026

In Church Road there are some older houses and the parish church; the south churchyard boundary runs along Church Lane to the left. St Helen's churchyard contains a great historical treasure: an Anglo-Saxon churchyard cross, the most important pre-Conquest monument in Nottinghamshire (right). Over ten feet high, with a protective hat-like capping of 1820, its date is uncertain, but it is probably 8th-century. The iron gates in the foreground came from Wellington College in 1922.

STAPLEFORD
The Sherwin Arms,
Derby Road c1955   S718015

The Nottingham to Derby main road, the A52, formerly passed through the centre of Stapleford, crossing The Roach (S718006, page 27). The 1960s by-pass reduced traffic in the heart of the town; it rejoins the route of the A52 at the Ilkeston Road junction, a large roundabout now just to the right of this view.
The Sherwin Arms, built in 1935 for Nottingham's Shipstone Brewery, is now accessed from a much quieter Derby Road, now relegated to B-road status.

STAPLEFORD, *The New School c1955*   S718036

Continuing eastwards along the A52 beyond The Sherwin Arms, we come to a complex of council schools, both primary and secondary, built in Bramcote Hill Park. The style is classic 1950s: rows of windows are surrounded by stone or concrete projecting jambs, heads and sills, as we can see on the first floor at the left. Bramcote Park School is now a comprehensive.

STAPLEFORD, *The Hemlock Stone c1955*   S718038

Our visit to Stapleford concludes with an oddity: the Hemlock Stone. This wind-eroded sandstone outcrop, about 30 feet high, is situated on the eastern edge of Stapleford Hill, just off the A6002 Coventry Lane. Needless to say, it has accumulated legends, including one that the Devil threw it at the now almost completely demolished Lenton Priory.

WEST BRIDGFORD
Central Avenue c1965   W437031

From Stapleford the route heads along the Trent to West Bridgford, south of the river and opposite Nottingham. Effectively a middle-class suburb of Nottingham, West Bridgford has the County Council offices of 1937 near the river; it also has Trent Bridge cricket ground, the home of Nottinghamshire County Cricket Club and a venue for test matches and internationals. This view, looking north with the trees of Bridgford Park on the right, shows an area further south than the river; Central Avenue is part of the main shopping centre.

WEST BRIDGFORD, *Central Avenue c1965*   W437016

Further back in Tudor Square, Frith's photographer was looking into Central Avenue with Albert Road to the right and Rectory Road to the left. The left-hand corner is occupied by an early 1960s Electricity Board building, nowadays Lunn Poly, and the Derbyshire Building Society. From 1931 until 1960 this site had been occupied by the Tudor Cinema, an extraordinary building with a tall timber-framed wing and a weird circular stone stair turret on its frontage.

WEST BRIDGFORD, *St Giles's Church c1960*   W437001

The core of the old village lies at the north end of Central Avenue, where the road becomes Bridgford Road. Here stands the Hall and the parish church of St Giles, where my uncle was married in August 1955. The tower and part of the south aisle are medieval. The rest, much larger in scale as befitted this now prosperous suburb, was started in 1896, and is a convincing essay in Perpendicular Gothic. This view looks through the Church Drive gateway towards the west tower.

WEST BRIDGFORD, *The Park c1960* W437013

East of the Central Avenue/Bridgford Road junction is Bridgford Park; the house's extensive grounds are now a very popular public park. The house itself, now the offices of Rushcliffe Borough Council's Social Services and the Register Office, was built in 1768-1774, but extended later. This view shows the south front; behind the house, in the northern half of the park, are tennis courts, sports fields and a car park.

RADCLIFFE ON TRENT
The Post Office and Main Road c1955
R310197

From suburban West Bridgford we move east along the A52 to Radcliffe, its village centre some 300 yards south of the River Trent. The village grew in the 19th century, and this is its predominant architectural character, with 20th-century suburbs and estates to the south and east. The post office is now a funeral director's. In the distance is the church of 1879, and in front of it is St Mary's Church Centre of 1876, now with modern flats between it and the baker's with the Hovis sign (centre).

▼ **RADCLIFFE ON TRENT,** *The Weir c1955* R310199

East of the village, the Shelford Road climbs on to the red sandstone hills, which are undercut by the River Trent to form river cliffs. The Trent Valley Way long-distance footpath runs through the cliff-top woods for over a mile. Leaving the path we can descend to the foot of the cliffs to this weir, and leaving the woods, walk back to the village along the river bank. This view is now somewhat obscured by a steel mesh security fence. The roaring waters of the weir are by-passed by Stoke Lock, out of view to the right.

▶ **BINGHAM**

Nottingham Road from Long Acre c1955 B651007

Four miles east of Radcliffe and across the A46 (which follows the course of the Roman road from Axminster to Lincoln, the Fosse Way), we reach Bingham, its western suburbs now reaching the A46 and also by-passed to the south by the busy A52. Here Frith's photographer was looking from Long Acre along the Nottingham Road, with early 19th-century cottages on the right and the first phases of 20th-century expansion, the 1930s semis, on the left. The White Lion remains, but not now offering Home Brewery's Fine Ales – this Nottingham brewery finally closed in 1996.

36

◀ **BINGHAM**
Market Street
c1955 B651005

Bingham is an ancient market town. After a long period of economic decline, it revived in the 19th century; but its architecture is drab, and much was demolished and rebuilt from the 1960s on as the town expanded. The two buildings on the left, for example, went in the 1960s, and their site became merely a car park for the rebuilt Co-op, which occupies much of the south side of the square. The Market Place has recently been pedestrianised and landscaped attractively around the 1861 Butter Cross; perhaps the tide has turned.

▶ **BINGHAM**
East Street c1955 B651010

From the Market Place, Church Street heads east; it has some good houses and cottages. At the Church Lane junction stands All Saints' church with its tower and spire of about 1300. This view is from east of the churchyard, in East Street, with the pedestrian path to Church Street behind the swan-necked lamp post. On the left is Church House, dated 1845, built as a school. The cottages in front of the church have been demolished and replaced by the 1960s neo-Georgian offices of J Enness & Co.

◀ **BURTON JOYCE**
The Wheatsheaf c1965
B606021

Accessed from both Main Street behind and from Church Road, the A612, behind the camera, the Wheatsheaf pub still thrives. Built in the 1930s in yellow brick, it also has areas of weatherboarding, and the terrace is still in use. Beyond we can see some of the 1950s houses fronting Main Street.

◄ **BURTON JOYCE**
Meadow Lane c1965
B606025

Re-crossing the Trent at Gunthorpe, the route turns back towards Nottingham along the busy A612 to Burton Joyce, where the river sweeps close to the road. The village has grown rapidly in the 20th century east and west along and parallel to the main road and northwards along the valley of a small stream. This view looks along Meadow Lane, which continues behind the photographer across Church Road, the A612, to the banks of the Trent. On the left is the flat-roofed 1960s Burton Joyce Library, and in the distance is Main Street.

▲ **BURTON JOYCE,** *The New School c1965*   B606005

Along Padleys Lane, which curves north out of the village amid 1950s and later estate houses, we pass Burton Joyce Primary School. This was built around 1960 using a system known as CLASP (Consortium of Local Authorities Special Programmes). It consists of a light steel frame on a fixed module that was clad in solid panels or glass as required. The school has recently been refurbished. The CLASP system was highly praised at the time; Nottinghamshire County Council's architects department used it for numerous schools all over the county.

◄ **BURTON JOYCE**
The Poplar Walk c1965
B606015

Main Street crosses Church Street, the A612, to become Station Road as far as the railway line, which runs between the village and the river. Beyond the still-functioning railway station, the lane reverts to its pre-railway name of Stoke Lane, and heads for the Trent between an avenue of fine Lombardy poplars. The hedge on the right has been replaced by a fence, but the poplars remain intact.

BURTON JOYCE
The River Trent c1965
B606016

A little further along Stoke Lane there is now a car park provided by the Stoke Bardolph Estate, owned by Severn Trent Water. From this car park we reach the banks of the River Trent where the footpath crosses a small stone bridge over a stream. There has been much planting in the foreground and beyond the gate, but the fine sweep of the view with Burton Joyce as a backdrop remains intact. The notice put up by the gate by the City of Nottingham bans vehicles and camping.

GEDLING, *Coronation Walk and Burton Road c1960*   G311009

Although they are outside the City of Nottingham's boundaries, Carlton and Gedling are really its eastern suburbs. This view was taken just east of the railway bridge over Burton Road, which led to the now-closed Arnold Colliery. The green now has five ash trees and a modern phone box. The houses on the left are part of the Coronation Walk estate, which was built soon after the coronation of Queen Elizabeth II in 1953. The shop is now an off-licence and convenience store.

GEDLING
Burton Road c1960
G311014

We are now west of the former colliery railway line bridge. Burton Road (left) was the main road until the southern by-pass, Colwick Loop Road, was built; its roundabout joined the old road at the far right of this view. It certainly took the pressure off Burton Road, although the houses here lost much of their front gardens to the new road. The park on the right is Burton Road Recreation Ground, now with modern pavilions.

GEDLING, *Main Road c1960*   G311022

Gedling is well known for the 14th-century spire of its parish church, about a quarter of a mile from where this picture was taken. There is very much a Victorian suburban feel here, apart from the 1950s concrete swan-necked lamp-post. The post office on the left is now a house; the post office has moved across the road into Read the tobacconist's next to the Gedling Wine Stores on the corner of Waverley Avenue – this shop is now Barber's Queue, a hairdresser's and sun bed tanning centre.

MANSFIELD TO EASTWOOD

MANSFIELD
The Market Place c1955   M184028

Mansfield lies some 14 miles north of Nottingham and to the west of Sherwood Forest. It is a town with sprawling suburbs and a centre marred by ring roads and the enormous Four Seasons Shopping Centre (1972-76), which demolished much of the northern part of the old town. However, there are good parts surviving on its hilly site, and the Market Place is thriving. This view was taken from beside the Town Hall of 1836, looking north to the corner of Westgate.

MANSFIELD
The Market Place c1955
M184034

From an upper window of the Town Hall, built unsurprisingly in Mansfield sandstone, the photographer looks across the Market Place to the elaborate Gothic canopied memorial to Lord George Bentinck, politician son of the Duke of Portland, who died suddenly at Welbeck Abbey in 1848. The pedimented building at the corner (left) is the 1752 former Moot Hall given by Lady Oxford, and another connection with Welbeck Abbey. All the buildings in this view survive more or less intact, and the Market Place is now largely pedestrianised.

MANSFIELD
St Peter's Church c1955
M184003

From the Market Place, descend Church Street to the parish church, passing under the great Mansfield sandstone railway viaduct of 1875 that marches across the town, neatly bisecting the old core. The church setting is somewhat marred by traffic sweeping past its north and west sides, decanted here by the recent pedestrianisation of the streets around the Market Place. This view looks north from the gates in Church Side; the left-hand tree hides the Norman lower part of the tower.

MANSFIELD, *Toothill Lane c1955*　M184014

Going back under the railway viaduct, we ascend Toothill Lane to its junction with Leeming Street, which crosses the foreground. The timber framing on the corner building is not genuine; it and the render conceal 18th- and 19th-century brick and stone houses (the furriers is now an estate agency). The two distant gables further downhill belong to the 1920s Handley Arcade, which passes behind the foreground buildings to emerge in Leeming Street, just out of view to the left, this time in a Classical columned stone garb.

MANSFIELD
Rock Dwellings c1955
M184025

The high quality Mansfield sandstone was quarried near the town and used widely - for example at Newark Town Hall in the 1770s. This view is taken up Rock Hill on the A617 Newark Road, approaching the crossroads with Carter Lane and Windsor Road, with the famous rock dwellings cut into the sandstone on the left. They were first mentioned in 1790, but are possibly older; only one was still occupied by 1894. They have now been entirely demolished on safety grounds.

NEWSTEAD ABBEY, *The Byron Tea Rooms c1955*   N29015

Newstead was inherited by the 'mad, bad and dangerous to know' poet Lord Byron in 1798 as a virtual ruin, and he sold it in 1817. A previous Lord Byron, the fifth, an ex-Naval man, had a warship in the lake and built mock forts around its edges in the 1770s; this one is the only survivor, and is in fact a conversion of the stables, which were subsequently extended to the right of the view in 1862. No longer tea rooms, they are now private houses partly screened by hedges.

NEWSTEAD ABBEY

Boatswain the Dog's Tomb c1955   N29013

Newstead Abbey has traded heavily on Lord Byron, although he managed little here in the way of repair - he even used the great hall as a shooting gallery. However, the house and its 300 acres of park were presented to the City of Nottingham in 1931, and major collections of Byron memorabilia were also given over the years, which are displayed in the house. Near the site of the priory church's high altar Byron erected this splendid tomb to his Newfoundland dog, Boatswain, who died in 1808 aged 5: a semi-sacrilegious act typical of the man.

NEWSTEAD ABBEY
*The Japanese Water Gardens
c1955* N29021

The Abbey (an Augustinian priory founded in the 1160s) was granted to the Byrons by Henry VIII in 1539, after the Dissolution. The house envelops much of the cloisters and the buildings surrounding them, and the great 13th-century abbey west front survives. A later owner, Mr Webb, a keen orientalist, created a Japanese water garden as well as rock and rose gardens. The Japanese Garden is currently being restored (2003).

HUCKNALL, *The Parish Church c1960* H373013

From Newstead Abbey the route heads four miles south to Hucknall, which also has Byronic associations: in this church Byron was buried in the family vault after his body had been brought home from Greece in 1824. St Mary Magdalene's church runs west from the Market Place and was heavily Victorianised and extended – the new chancel's foundation stone was laid by the Duke of Portland in 1887. The medieval tower is the oldest part of the church now, but the churchyard is a haven of green in the town centre.

▼ **HUCKNALL,** *Co-operative House c1960* H373016

Hucknall, surrounded by coal mining villages and with its own sprawling suburbs, grew greatly in Victorian times but did not acquire much architecture of distinction. The north side of the Market Place (still a car park) was dominated by the Co-op, which expanded into the right-hand corner building of 1898. The statue in the niche on the left is of Byron. Currently (2003) all the buildings are being refurbished as flats over shops, and renamed, of course, the Byron Centre.

▶ **HUCKNALL,** *Titchfield Park c1960* H373020

Titchfield Park lies east of Park Drive, south of the town centre, towards Broomhill, and surrounded by suburban semi-detached houses. Laid out in the late 19th century, it is an attractive well-treed park with sports pitches, avenues and a bowling green, which we see here from the south-west - it is now enclosed by green railings. Through the trees on the right we can just see the high pedestal of the war memorial of the early 1920s.

◀ **EASTWOOD**
Nottingham Road
1955   E183004

Eastwood is, of course, famous as the birthplace and home of D H Lawrence. This view from the Mansfield Road junction looks uphill along Nottingham Road, the principal shopping street, lined by mostly 19th-century buildings. To the left of the car, by the white painted building, is the entrance to Victoria Street, where in No 8a D H Lawrence was born on 11 September 1885. The house, a two-up, two-down and attic, is now a museum which spreads into the shop next door, on the corner of the evocatively named Scargill Street.

▶ **EASTWOOD**
Nottingham Road c1955
E183002

We are looking downhill from the east, and the entrance to D H Lawrence's Victoria Street can be seen half-way down on the right by the white building. The church on the right with the spire, the Congregational chapel, was where D H Lawrence first met Jessie Chambers of Haggs Farm. Unfortunately (and perhaps unsurprisingly in relation to the scandals Lawrence provoked), the church was demolished in the 1960s; the site is now occupied by a freezer centre, a single-storey flat-roofed building.

▲ EASTWOOD
Nottingham Road c1955   E183015

Further along Nottingham Road, Frith's photographer looks eastwards towards Hill Top with the junction with Edward Road between the hedge and the wall. At this corner stands a war memorial to the Eastwood men who served in the Sherwood Foresters regiment during World War I. Part of the hedge is now railings, but the row of Lombardy poplars survive, now more mature, and so does the plane tree (right).

▶ EASTWOOD
Hill Top c1960   E183017

Just past the junction with Dovecote Road, at Hill Top, the road descends to the valley of the Gilt Brook and to Nottingham some eight miles away. On the right is the dull red brick Roman Catholic church of Our Lady of Good Counsel. It and the housing all survive, though not a single dwelling retains its original windows. The house beyond the church is now the Hilltop Haven Residential Home.

EASTWOOD, *Beauvale School c1955*   E183006

Turning into Dovecote Road we wind half a mile east to the corner of Mill Road to finish this chapter on a literary note. Erected as the Greasley Board School in 1878, it is now named Greasley Beauvale D H Lawrence Infant School. The door at the far left has the inscription 'Boys' above it, so through this door young D H Lawrence entered in 1893, aged 8. It is a little ironic that the town D H Lawrence offended so much by *Sons and Lovers* now commemorates him, and even has a D H Lawrence Trail.

NEWARK, SOUTHWELL AND THE EASTERN TRENT VALLEY

NEWARK-ON-TRENT
The View from St Mary's Church Tower c1965   N12060

Newark grew up where the Roman road from Axminster to Lincoln met the medieval Great North Road's predecessor and crossed the River Trent. The name is Danish, meaning 'new fortress', and the strategic importance of the river crossing defended by river cliffs is emphasised by the castle. This unusual view looks north-west from the tower of St Mary Magdalene's church across the pantiled and slate roofs of the town; the streets and lanes are mostly as laid out by Alexander, Bishop of Lincoln in the early 12th century. To the right is the castle, with the River Trent below and the water meadows beyond.

NEWARK-ON-TRENT
The Castle c1955 N12013

Bishop Alexander's castle was started in the 1130s, but much of what we see now is 14th-century. Once known as 'the Key to the North', the castle had a chequered history: King John died here in 1216, and in the Civil War it endured three long sieges in the 1640s - the town was staunchly Royalist. After this the castle was ordered to be demolished, but fortunately the long walls to the river front and half of the east wall largely survived. This view is in the public gardens formed within the castle bailey after the corporation bought the castle in 1889, and shows the gatehouse (right).

NEWARK-ON-TRENT, *Trent Bridge c1955* N12052

Seen from the north-west bank of the River Trent, the castle appears foreshortened; but the wall in this view is that half of the east curtain wall that survived the 1650s demolition, with the gatehouse at the left. The present stone bridge replaced earlier ones (the first built in timber by the energetic Bishop Alexander in the 12th century); it dates from 1775, with footways and cast iron railings added in 1848. The town is now by-passed by both the A1 Great North Road, which crossed the bridge, and the Fosse Way (the A46).

▶ **NEWARK-ON-TRENT**
Market Square c1955
N12008

At the heart of Bishop Alexander's town was the large market place into which the Fosse Way was diverted, although none of the buildings in this view are medieval. The pedimented building is Carr of York's Town Hall of 1773 built in local Mansfield sandstone; the ground floor meat market is now a shopping arcade, the Butter Market. Curry's to the right is now an antiques centre. The building on the right side of the square with the white quoins is the Moot Hall of 1708, rebuilt in replica in 1967.

◀ **NEWARK-ON-TRENT**
Ye Olde White Hart c1955
N12006

In the south-east corner of the Market Square is its only surviving timber-framed building, Ye Olde White Hart, a superb and rich example of late 15th-century building. Dilapidated for some years, it has now been beautifully restored, with the timber painted in many colours in an authentic reconstruction of a medieval colour scheme. The ground floor to the left is now an entrance to a shopping arcade, and the right-hand shop is now a Nottingham Building Society office. George Mason, the 'Largest Grocers in the Midlands', is now a Boots opticians.

▲ **NEWARK-ON-TRENT,** *The Old Governor's House, Stodman Street c1955* N12037

Stodman Street leads out of the south-west corner of the Market Place. Its most famous building is the Governor's House, a 16th-century timber-framed house with three storeys of coved jetties. It has survived relatively unchanged because of its historical associations with the Civil War; it was the residence of the Royalist governor, and a plaque informs us that the dashing cavalry leader Prince Rupert stayed here in 1645. It is now a Bakers Oven shop.

◄ **NEWARK-ON-TRENT**
Stodman Street c1955 N12035

Newark enjoyed great prosperity in the 18th century through industrial growth and through its status as a coaching town on the Great North Road. There was much rebuilding then, so the town has a predominantly Georgian character; there was further rebuilding after the railway, the east coast main line, arrived in the 1840s. The town plan is still that of the medieval town, but there has been 20th-century rebuilding. Much of the middle distance was rebuilt in the 1970s, and the little pantile-roofed medieval building (right) went in the 1960s.

NEWARK-ON-TRENT
Bridge Street c1955 N12032

All survives in Bridge Street, which leads out of the south-east side of the Market Place in the distance. These are Georgian and early 19th-century buildings; the lower pedimented building, Morris's (right), is a two-storey early 19th-century building, despite a 1950s attempt to give it a modern screen. The shop blinds have gone since the 1950s. The taller building at the right-hand corner, early 18th-century, is now G H Porter, 'Provisions', but in 1806-07 this was where Lord Byron's first volumes of poetry were published.

NEWARK-ON-TRENT
Appleton Gate c1955
N12031

Bridge Street leads into Carter Gate and Appleton Gate, 'gate' being the Viking word for street. Appleton Gate heads north-east past the rear of the parish churchyard, its location marked by the steps and the tall tree. The shop on the left is still a newsagent, Church Walk Newsagents. Good Georgian buildings on the right give way to the Palace Theatre, now painted in various shades of green. Built in the 1920s, it has exotic Indian onion-domed turrets, and is still a thriving theatre.

NEWARK-ON-TRENT, *Barnby Gate c1955*   N12027

Going back to the Bridge Street junction, the tour heads south-west down Cartergate, a street somewhat marred by insensitive modern rebuilding, and turns into Barnby Gate (Cartergate is in the distance). The high building on the left was rebuilt in the 1960s; beyond is the Imperial Hall, which runs through to Balderton Gate to the west. The Rutland Arms Hotel (right) is still in business, and so is The White Horse, the smaller building beyond.

NEWARK-ON-TRENT, *Balderton Gate c1955* N12029

Balderton Gate is the next turning south-east off Cartergate. Here we have a glimpse of the 237 feet high spire of St Mary Magdalene's. The rendered gable on the right belongs to the Imperial Hall, now the Imperial Snooker Club and Lightning Jack's Nite Club. The painted advertisement extolling the virtues of Robb's pork pies and sausages (left) can still be put to the test, as Robb's is still in the same shop.

► **NEWARK-ON-TRENT**
Beaumond Cross
c1965 N12093

Beaumond Cross is still a busy junction at the south-west end of Carter Gate, emerging by the newsagents advertising the News of the World (right, still a newsagent). The road to the left is Lombard Gate, and the white car is emerging from London Road. Widening and road improvements led to the 15th-century wayside preaching cross behind the concrete lamp post being removed to London Road Gardens in 1974. Note the graceful spire of St Mary Magdalene's towering over the townscape.

◄ **NEWARK-ON-TRENT**
The Great North Road and the Castle c1955 N12007

London Road, the old A1 before the town was by-passed, becomes Lombard Street before turning right into Castle Gate with its many former coaching inns; it then turns left beyond the castle to cross the River Trent. This seems a quiet day, for my childhood memories of passing through Newark are of nose-to-tail crawls and relief on crossing the bridge. This spacious boulevard is in fact Beast Market Hill, and was just that in years past. On the right is the former Ossington Coffee Palace.

▲ **NEWARK-ON-TRENT,** *The Ossington Coffee Palace c1965* N12111

The Palace, designed by the illustrious London architects Ernest George & Peto and built in 1882 at the then enormous cost of £20,000, was funded by Viscountess Ossington, sister of the 5th Duke of Portland of Welbeck Abbey. A hundred-year covenant banned alcohol. As well as the coffee tavern, the building provided clubrooms, a library and a bowling alley to distract the citizens from the Demon Drink. Not a great success in a town full of inns and taverns, it became offices, but much of the ground floor is now a Zizzi's restaurant.

◀ **NEWARK-ON-TRENT**
Town Lock and the Castle c1965 N12090

Newark is a town with a wealth of historic buildings, and it is relatively little changed compared with Grantham or even Nottingham. This view is from the Town Lock on the River Trent, which was built in 1951 to accommodate 250-ton boats; its smaller and narrower predecessor lies on the far right. The castle is framed by an inelegant pipe-carrying bridge, now gone, but it frames the castle well. The weir it by-passes is out of view to the left.

▼ **SOUTHWELL,** *The Minster c1955* S564035

The route leaves Newark and heads six miles west to the small and delightful town of Southwell, whose minster church had been founded by the Archbishop of York before AD956. The Archbishop's Palace partly survives. The present minster church, which dominates the town, was begun in about 1108, and the Norman nave, transepts and west towers survive. The Norman east end was rebuilt later in the Middle Ages. The minster became a cathedral in 1884. In this view from Westgate the conical trees survive.

▶ **SOUTHWELL**
Market Place c1955 S564026

This view from the junction of Westgate with Church Street and Market Place looks past the Saracen's Head, a 16th-century timber-framed inn in which Charles I spent his last night of freedom in May 1646 before surrendering to Parliamentary forces (it was at that time The King's Head). Since the 1950s the stucco which had been applied in 1693 to the first floor has been stripped off to reveal the timber-framing beneath.

◄ **SOUTHWELL**
*The Saracen's
Head Yard c1955*
S564010

Frith's photographer
was looking back
through the
carriageway
towards Church
Street straight
ahead. These long
timber-framed
ranges remain, the
space between now
filled with pub
tables and benches,
while the rear of the
yard is now the
hotel car park. To
the right is now a
1990s extension to
the Methodist
church of 1839.

► **SUTTON-ON-TRENT**
The River Trent c1955 S236005

From Southwell the tour heads
north-east back to the River
Trent north of Newark and on to
Sutton-on-Trent. The village lies
just off the old Great North Road,
whose dual carriageway
successor passes it half a mile to
the west. This view shows the
banks of the Trent from a path
through the water meadows,
which were drained in the 1850s.
Cattle still graze here, but
beyond the left-hand dredging
barges the view north is now
dominated by the cooling towers
and chimneys of High Marnham
Power Station, opened in 1962.

SUTTON-ON-TRENT, *Church Street c1955* S236016

Church Street, seen here from the end of Main Street, with the High Street meeting it from the left, leads past the parish church of All Saints, one of Nottinghamshire's best parish churches. In this view all is obscured except the tower, which was rebuilt in 1902. Badgers Lair, the cottage on the left, has had its brickwork roughcast and colour-washed and the windows replaced by leaded lights since the 1950s, while the former shop beyond has also been drastically altered.

SUTTON-ON-TRENT
Main Street c1955 S236018

The church tower pinnacles are just visible above the trees. There has been much change here. Until the 1950s, Sutton was big enough to support a number of shops; however, many of these have closed, and the buildings have been converted to houses, including Woolfit House on the right and the Barber's Shop on the left in the foreground. The shop beyond, by the man in the cap, is now Sutton-on-Trent branch library, but the furthest building is still a butcher's shop, Colin Illsley.

SUTTON-ON-TRENT, *High Street c1955* S236011

The next four views were taken in the High Street, which runs westward to Hemplands Lane with the site of the railway station beyond. On the right is the Old England Hotel with its AA sign, built in the 1920s to cater for motorists and tourists using the Great North Road. It is a quirky building in leaded light vernacular style, and the boundary wall has milestones set in giving distances to Edinburgh, London and York.

SUTTON-ON-TRENT
High Street c1955 S236017

Past the Old England Hotel, the building on the right is now a house, its origins given away in its name, The Old Co-op. The shop on the left no longer sells Farmers Weekly; now a house, it has been roughcast and colour-washed, a common 'improvement' in the village. The cottage beyond was altered between 1955 and the date of view S236022 (page 70), with wider windows and concrete roof tiles.

▼ **SUTTON-ON-TRENT,** *High Street c1960* S236022

Further up the High Street, the whitewashed cottage on the right is called Kinver Edge. Beyond it is the Methodist church of 1878, which has a reused date stone of 1821 from the earlier Wesleyan chapel. The 1821 chapel, the hipped pantile-roofed building further along the road, itself survives. The shop with the gabled front beside it is now (2003) boarded up and empty; we can see it more clearly in S236008 (below).

▶ **SUTTON-ON-TRENT**
High Street c1955
S236008

Much has changed in this view. The farm buildings on the left have given way to modern houses, and there is a pavement on the right. The cycle shop (right) is now closed and unused (2003). Beyond is a closer view of the former Wesleyan chapel of 1821, its ground floor openings blocked and the ghost of its date plaque visible. The pantiled roofs beyond belong to the village smithy, now redeveloped with a cul-de-sac of houses

◀ SUTTON-ON-TRENT
The Railway c1955
S236010

An evocative photograph: an LNER steam locomotive hauls a train of wagons through Sutton-on-Trent station. The view is taken from the 1950s by-pass bridge which took the A1 past the village; the old road passed in front of The Nag's Head pub on the right, and is now named Old Great North Road. The modern A1 follows a new route half a mile to the west, so the village is quieter now. The steam engines have departed, of course, and the station has utterly vanished, although the east coast main line itself remains.

▶ EAST MARKHAM
The Village and the Church
c1955 E168007

We move north-west to East Markham, a village a mile or so east of the Great North Road. The modern A1 dual carriageway passes closer to the village now, and the church is even more prominent in views from that road. It is a village with many quiet lanes, with the 15th-century church of St John the Baptist at its southern edge and gently rolling countryside beyond. The farm buildings on the right have been replaced by bungalows, but those on the left remain, including Church Farm with its white Victorian porch.

WORKSOP AND THE DUKERIES

WORKSOP, *The Priory Church c1965* W278077

The fourth tour starts in Worksop, the largest town in north Nottinghamshire, often seen as the gateway to the Dukeries. We start at Worksop's finest building, the priory, formerly known as Radford Priory. The medieval town was at its gates, but moved westwards to its present location. The priory was founded around 1120. The present nave dates from the later 12th century, and of the abbey's east end only the superb Lady Chapel survives. The transepts with their two storeys of arches date from the 1920s and 1930s, while a modern central tower with a slender spire and a choir was erected from 1966 to 1974 by Laurence King.

▲ **WORKSOP**
The Priory Gatehouse c1955   W278051

Of the priory buildings, only the mid 14th-century gatehouse survives, with the medieval market cross in front. To the right of the central archway a delicate and elegant 14th-century porch led to a small chapel within. It was restored in 1912 at a cost of £550 and again in the 1940s, this time at a cost of £9,500. It is a fortunate survival, and gives some idea of the size of the priory's grounds, as the church is some distance away.

◄ **WORKSOP**
The War Memorial c1955   W278039

The priory became the parish church after its dissolution in the reign of Henry VIII, and the great east end and almost all the abbey buildings were pulled down. In the 1920s the war memorial was built to form the centrepiece of Memorial Avenue, leading from the town to the west front of the priory. The war memorial, a distinguished Baroque piece, was built before the avenue was anywhere near complete; it was unveiled by Sir Horace Smith-Dorrien, a veteran World War I general, in May 1925.

▼ **WORKSOP,** *The Library and Memorial Gardens c1955*   W278033

War Memorial Gardens were laid out to the north of Memorial Avenue between it and the Canch, as this stretch of the River Ryton is known. This view looks from the Canch banks towards the modernist library. It was built in the 1930s with a shallow central dome of glass blocks set in concrete, which lights the central space of the Central Library and Museum.

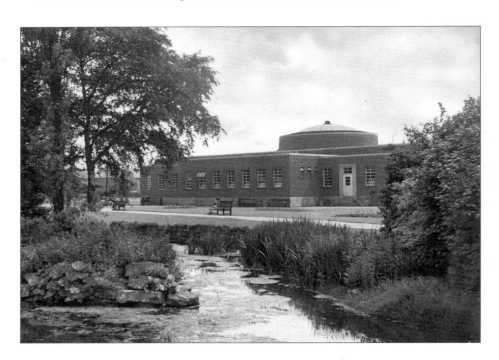

▶ **WORKSOP**

*Memorial Gardens and
the Priory Church c1955*
W278055

Now within the Memorial Gardens beyond the library, Frith's photographer was looking towards the west facade of Worksop Priory with its tall 12th-century towers, topped by 15th-century battlements and pinnacles. It was good for later generations that the parish kept their nave after the priory was suppressed.

◀ **WORKSOP**
Canch Walk c1955
W278032

Along the north bank of the Canch is a footpath that leads east to Priorswell Road, with the Memorial Gardens on the right bank behind the trees that line it. The rather temporary-looking chain link fence has been replaced by proper railings. The very tall tree in the middle distance conceals the site of Priory Mill, an old watermill. By 1900 it had ceased milling corn and was a timber yard and chair maker's workshop, but it burned down completely in 1912. Only a few walls survive to surround the Memorial Gardens maintenance yard.

▶ **WORKSOP**
Bridge Place c1965 W278087

After the glories of Worksop Priory and its medieval gatehouse, the town is more workaday, but many Georgian buildings survive. It is divided in two by the small River Ryton and the more substantial Chesterfield Canal, opened in the 1770s. This view looks south into Bridge Street from Bridge Place, with the1950s Co-operative House at the junction with Watson Road. This and the white gabled building were rebuilt, rather blandly, in the 1990s, while on the right in the middle distance much demolition took place for the rather poor 1970s Priory Shopping Centre.

WORKSOP
Bridge Street 1967 W278093

Now further down Bridge Street, Frith's photographer was looking south uphill past the Newcastle Street crossroads. Beyond the mainly Victorian buildings in the foreground are some good Georgian ones further uphill, such as the stone-built Lion Hotel on the far right. The road is now partly pedestrianised, and leads to the Market Place and the 1851 Town Hall, which was originally built as the corn exchange.

▶ **WORKSOP**
Victoria Square c1955
W278041

From Bridge Street we head north towards Victoria Square over the Chesterfield Canal, whose bridge parapets are in the foreground. Out of view to the right and spanning the canal is the former Pickford's Depository, a warehouse built in the early 19th century in yellow brick (the rest of the town is in red brick). It has trap doors for direct loading into the narrow barges, or 'cuckoos' as they were known, and a crane on the canal bank. It is now part of the Lock Tavern, which fronts the road.

◄ **WORKSOP**
Gateford Road c1965
W278089

Beyond Victoria Square the
town expanded along
Gateford Road and Carlton
Road towards the railway
station, which opened in
1850; it is stone-built in a
Jacobean style. The young
plane tree in the square has
now matured. In the distance
is the spire of St John the
Evangelist's, completed in
1868 to serve the expanded
north of the town. To the left
the Shopping Centre
occupied the Victoria Palace
Theatre; this was mainly used
as a cinema, and by the date
of this photograph had been
stripped of its ornate stucco
facings. Nowadays (2003) it is
a furniture shop.

◀ **WORKSOP**
Worksop College c1965
W278094

South of the town, beyond the modern A57 by-pass, accessed via a long avenue from the Netherton Road, is Worksop College. The school still thrives as a public school, nowadays taking girls as well as boys. It opened in 1895 as St Cuthbert's College, and was the sixth of the public schools founded by Nathaniel Woodard (Lancing College in Sussex was another). The buildings were mostly by R H Carpenter, although the grandly scaled chapel is by Aston Webb, and was added around 1910. My uncle was a pupil here before World War II.

◄ **WORKSOP**
Gateford Road
c1955 W278021

Further north along Gateford Road, near the Gladstone Street turn, the spire of St John the Evangelist's can be seen on the right behind the tall three-storey terrace of 1870s shops. To the right is the former Gateford Stores of 1905 in red brick and terra cotta, designed in a sort of Jacobean/Flemish style. It is now a carpet shop, having by the 1950s become a furniture store.

▲ **WORKSOP,** *The Lion Gates, Welbeck Abbey, c1965* W278059

Near the entrance to Worksop College, on Sparrow Hill (the old road into Worksop), are the lion gates and one of the many lodges and gateways into the vast 3,000 acre grounds of Welbeck Abbey, built for the Dukes of Portland. It is one of the Dukeries, as this part of Nottinghamshire has been called since the 18th century. This view of the 1894 gates was taken from within the grounds, with the corner of the lodge on the left.

◄ **WORKSOP**
Welbeck Abbey c1955
W278044

This vast and architecturally complex mansion is on the site of an abbey founded in 1153, of which fragments remain. After the Dissolution it eventually passed in 1597 to William Cavendish, grandson of the famous Bess of Hardwick, and then by marriage to the Dukes of Portland in 1734. Having for some years partly been occupied by an army college, it is now a private house, the home of William Parente, Prince of Castel Viscardo, a grandson of the 7th Duke of Portland.

CLUMBER PARK
The Bridge c1955 C500001

The second great ducal estate of the Dukeries was Clumber, now owned by the National Trust. The estate was given to the Duke of Newcastle in 1707, and is about 3,800 acres. The mansion was built in 1770 and vastly extended in the 19th century. It was demolished in 1938, leaving the 18th- and 19th-century stable blocks (now the National Trust Regional Office and visitors' centre) and the impressive church of the 1880s with its tall spire. This elegant bridge of 1763 spans the northern arm of the vast lake, which was mostly formed in the 1770s.

CLUMBER PARK *c1955* C500008

Clumber Park, like Rufford, is heavily wooded; it was enclosed out of Sherwood Forest, that great forest that extends from Worksop southwards almost to Nottingham. The soil is thin, sandy and infertile, but it suits slow-growing oak trees, birch and bracken. Of the Clumber estate's 3,800 acres over a thousand are woodland, while the great lake itself occupies 87 acres.

OLLERTON
Thoresby Hall c1965 O131054

South of Clumber the tour reaches a third great estate in the Dukeries, Thoresby: its great park was enclosed in the 1680s. This great mansion is the third one. The first, built in 1685 by Talman, burned down in 1745, and the second, by Carr of York and built in 1767, was felt to be rather too small for a man of the third Earl Manvers' status. It was replaced by one closer in scale to those of his ducal rivals at Clumber and Welbeck. The architect was Anthony Salvin, and work started on this great neo-Tudor pile in 1865.

OLLERTON, *Thoresby Hall, The Great Hall c1955* O131042

This view in Anthony Salvin's towering Great Hall was taken just before the last Earl Manvers, the sixth earl, died in 1955. The hall is on the first floor and three storeys high: a truly monumental space, here still furnished as the Manvers' family home. The grand double-flight staircases can be seen through the arcades with galleries overlooking the hall.

▶ **OLLERTON**
*Thoresby Hall, the Library
Chimneypiece c1960*
O131045

The main suite of rooms is south of the Great Hall. The library has an ornate chimneypiece carved in oak by a highly skilled carver from Mansfield. The overmantel panel shows the Major Oak (E142030, on page 89) from Sherwood Forest, while the figures on either side of the fireplace are Robin Hood on the left and Little John on the right. Sherwood Forest in which Thoresby sits is, of course, the heart of Robin Hood country.

OLLERTON, *Thoresby Hall, the Queen Victoria Room c1965*   O131050

This plainer room is one occupied by Queen Victoria when she stayed at Thoresby, enjoying the lavish hospitality of Earl Manvers. The house itself is no longer the residence of the heirs to the extinct earldom; it has recently been bought and fully restored as one of Warner Holidays Ltd's Historic Hotels. To the north of the house Warner's have built a brick and stone-dressed bedroom block and a spa and health club.

OLLERTON

Thoresby Hall, the Robin Hood Statue c1955 O131039

The eastern front is approached through a fine screen of iron railings and gate piers, and at the centre of this forecourt is a statue of Robin Hood drawing his bow. The statue has been retained by Warner Holidays Limited, and is now surrounded by roses up to Robin's waist.

◄ **OLLERTON**

Thoresby Hall, the Model Railway Engine c1965 O131095

Although in the 1960s still occupied by Earl Manvers' heirs, the mansion and grounds were open to the public - in O131054 (page 83) we can see the ticket booth for those who wished to look inside the house. There were many attractions for visitors, including the miniature railway. Here we see a working model of one of the great engineer Sir Nigel Gresley's streamlined Pacific locomotives built for the LNER in the 1930s - this one was named after him.

► **BUDBY**
The Village c1955
B833021

To the west of Thoresby, on the Ollerton to Worksop road, the first Earl Manvers of Thoresby built a small estate village around 1810. Designed by William Wilkins, the houses were fairly plain, with rendered elevations; the only elaboration was Gothic tracery timber windows and some bow windows and porches. The one on the right, North Farm House, has had its farm buildings converted into the Dukeries Antiques Centre. The stream is the River Meden, which feeds into Thoresby's enormous ornamental lake.

◄ **OLLERTON**
The Dukeries, Old Ollerton Church c1955 O131008

Ollerton village was at the crossroads of three major routes, and its inns catered for the coaching trade, but now, mercifully, it is by-passed and tranquil. New Ollerton immediately north-east is a large mining village that grew up around Thoresby Colliery. Old Ollerton's church was rebuilt in 1780 in Gothic style; it is now more visible, as two of the trees have since gone. The churchyard wall has also been repaired and partly rebuilt.

▲ **OLLERTON,** *The Dukeries, the Hop Pole Hotel c1955* O131005

North-east of the church is the Hop Pole Hotel, a good 18th-century coaching inn that also catered for visitors to the great Dukeries mansions. Nearby are two other inns, The White Hart and The Snooty Fox. Beyond is Ollerton Hall, late 17th-century and derelict for some years, but shortly to become a Sue Ryder Home. There is also a working watermill with an iron water wheel powered by the River Maun, and an accompanying tea room.

◄ **OLLERTON**
Rufford Abbey c1955
O131016

South of Ollerton is Rufford Country Park, run by the County Council. The abbey was founded in 1136; it was converted into a house and further enlarged in the 17th century by the Savile family. It was bought by the County Council as a crumbling ruin; the large early 18th-century block at the left was demolished in 1956. Much of the remainder is roofless, but restored and consolidated; the Country Park was opened in 1969, and very popular it is too, with a café and shops in the nearby stable block.

OLLERTON, *Sherwood Forest c1955* O131014

Sherwood Forest once covered over 100,000 acres between Nottingham and Worksop, although the great ducal estates of the Dukeries enclosed much of the north part for their parks. As early as the 10th century, this vast tract of wooded landscape was known as 'sher wood', meaning 'the wood belonging to the county or shire', and by the 12th century it was a royal forest subject to its own Forest Law. This view is in the Sherwood Forest Country Park, an area of 450 acres with many of the best surviving ancient oak trees amid silver birch, younger oaks and bracken.

EDWINSTOWE
The Major Oak c1960
E142030

At the heart of the Sherwood Forest Country Park is the famous Major Oak, about half a mile west of the modern Visitor Centre. This ancient oak, completely hollow, is probably over 700 years old; it is now fenced off, and its heavy old boughs are propped up. It acquired its name not from its size or status, although it has a girth of about 33 feet, but from a Major Rooke, an antiquarian who described it in 1790. Before Major Rooke's interest the tree was known as the Queen Oak.

EDWINSTOWE, *Sherwood Forest c1955* E142011

Here we have another view of a track in the forest. Here we might catch glimpses of fallow deer and even roe and red deer. The area is, of course, always associated with the deeds of Robin Hood and his Merry Men and their struggles with the Sheriff of Nottingham; but the earliest tales of Robin are set in Yorkshire, and the stories only move him to Nottinghamshire in later ballads and tales.

▼ **EDWINSTOWE,** *The Church c1960* E142018

Described as 'Robin Hood's village', Edwinstowe lies south of the Sherwood Forest Country
Park. An Anglo-Saxon settlement grew up around the chapel on the site of the grave of
Edwin, King of Northumberland. He had been killed at the Battle of Heathfield in AD633.
The present rather good church with its largely 19th-century spire is mostly 12th- and 13th-
century; reputedly, Robin Hood and Maid Marian were married in this church's predecessor
by, of course, Friar Tuck.

▶ **EDWINSTOWE**
High Street c1955 E142004

The High Street is a somewhat
disappointingly disjointed
one architecturally. Several
buildings were funded by Earl
Manvers, including an
institute (now an Adult
Education Centre) of 1913 and
the Co-op of 1895. Beyond the
late 19th-century Dutch
gabled Ye Olde Jug and Glass
on the left, the white gable
and pantile roof belong to the
Black Swan Inn, a recently
somewhat mutilated building
apparently of 15th-century
date. The two gabled cottages
in the foreground have been
replaced since the 1950s.

◄ **EDWINSTOWE**
High Street c1955
E142014

This view looks north along the High Street past the now 'improved' junction with West Lane. The Mansfield, Sutton and District Co-operative Society shop on the corner (left) was funded by Earl Manvers in 1895. This has now been replaced by a 1960s version of little merit; its building involved demolishing the house beyond. In the middle distance on the right are the pantiled roofs of the now altered Black Swan Inn.

► **EDWINSTOWE**
The Dukeries Hotel c1955
E142005

Downhill to the south and across the River Maun, the High Street continues uphill to pass The Dukeries Hotel, now for some reason called Ma Hubbard's Eating House and Hotel. This half-timbered building with its many gables was built in 1895 for the Mansfield Brewery at a cost of £543. Since the 1950s the porch has been converted into a stone-built bow window. The hotel served both the community (which had grown greatly in the 19th century after the colliery was opened) and railway travellers, for it stands near where the pre-Beeching station was.

EAST RETFORD AND THE FAR NORTH

EAST RETFORD, *Market Square c1955* R261078

The tour now reaches the northern part of the county, perhaps the least visited part of Nottinghamshire. The largest towns are Worksop and East Retford – Worksop was covered in Chapter 4. East Retford has at its heart a market place, first chartered in 1246. The stalls are nowadays roofed in smart blue- and pink-banded awnings, and surround the war memorial, which was erected in 1921.

93

► **EAST RETFORD**
Market Square
c1955 R261031

Since 1977 the market square has been pedestrianised on non-market days, but until the A1 bypassed the town in the 1960s the Great North Road from London to Edinburgh streamed along its east side. Ironically, the old Great North Road had been diverted in 1766 so that East Retford could benefit economically from the coaching trade and commerce, while the canal further boosted the town's prosperity.

◄ **EAST RETFORD**
Market Square c1965
R261044

The railway (in the 1950s the LNER's east coast main line) brought further prosperity; this included the building of a new town hall in the 1860s, seen here with its clock tower. It looks more like an ornate bank. Indeed, the borough offices expanded into the neighbouring Old Bank in 1926, the hard red terracotta building to the right of 1887. The ancient borough was absorbed into Bassetlaw District Council in 1974.

▲ **EAST RETFORD,** *Cannon Square c1955* R261028

Frith's photographer was outside St Swithun's churchyard, looking through Cannon Square towards the south-east arm of the Market Square and the 18th-century White Hart. The cannon was captured at Sebastopol in 1855 and mounted here in 1859, when the area was renamed Cannon Square. During World War II it and the distinctive iron railings were dismantled and stored, thus escaping being melted down for Spitfires, and reinstated in 1949. Much of the distant area is now pedestrianised.

◀ **EAST RETFORD**
Moorgate c1960 R261051

Moorgate runs towards Cannon Square, and the trees belong to the churchyard - the pinnacled tower of St Swithun's church rises on the left. However, since this view was taken, East Retford's inner relief road, Arlington Way, has been cut across the foreground; the three shops to the left of the Sherwood Rangers Inn, now simply The Sherwood Ranger, were demolished. The pub has since lost its arched gable.

EAST RETFORD
Grove Street c1960   R261038

Grove Street runs east from the Market Square, a mix of 18th- and 19th-century buildings, and a mix of shops and houses. Several of the houses are 18th-century, and are occupied, as in most small towns, by solicitors, including the one on the left with the bow windows. In the distance is the domineering 1000-seater Methodist church of 1880; it is by the same architect as the Town Hall, and in a similarly overblown style.

EAST RETFORD
Carolgate c1955
R261037

Much has changed in this view looking north along Carolgate towards the Market Place past the junction with Exchange Street. The building on the far left and B & M Lingerie (right) have been replaced in the 1980s; so has the building beyond the London Central Meat Company on the left (now a phone shop with a decidedly poorer modern shop front than the Edwardian one seen here). The street has also been pedestrianised as part of the recent town centre improvements.

▶ **EAST RETFORD**
Trinity Hospital
c1955 R261020

The village of West Retford, with its own medieval parish church, St Michael's, lies on the west bank of the River Idle, and has long been absorbed into the town. Holy Trinity Hospital stands opposite the mainly 1669 West Retford Hall. Almshouses rather than a hospital in the modern sense, it was founded in 1671 and rebuilt in the 1820s with a central chapel of 1872. Until the 1970s, the elderly residents or 'brethren' wore cloaks when out and about in the town.

◀ **EAST RETFORD**
The Chesterfield Canal
c1955 R261014

A little further along Hospital Road the Chesterfield Canal passes under the road; the bridge was rebuilt some thirty years ago. This view looks towards the bridge from below West Retford Lock, and beyond is Bettison Wharf, the pantile-roofed late 18th-century canal warehouse. This has now gone, to be replaced by the caretaker's house for the Elizabethan High School, whose grounds are behind the fence on the left.

◄ **EAST RETFORD**
The Sir Frederick Milner School c1955 R261018

The Sir Frederick Milner School was built as a secondary modern school in the south-east of the town, amid a maze of narrow streets. In 1977, when the schools of Retford became comprehensive, it was renamed King Edward VI School, merging with the original grammar school which had been founded in the 1550s in Edward VI's reign. Rebuilt on London Road in the 1850s, the old grammar school buildings survive as the other campus of Edward VI School after the merger with the Milner.

BARNBY MOOR
Ye Olde Bell Hotel c1955
B607009

Four miles north-west of East Retford, the Great North Road (A1) reaches Barnby Moor. Here the 1766 diversion through the town rejoins the old route, now a minor road heading south and named Old London Road. Beyond the junction is the famous Old Bell, an important coaching inn from at least the 17th century. The A1 no longer goes through Barnby Moor, but is a modern dual carriageway a mile to the west. Ye Olde Bell is little changed apart from the loss of the huge bell at the gable.

BARNBY MOOR, *The Wiseton Room, Ye Olde Bell Hotel c1955* B607014

Ye Olde Bell was described in the 18th century as a 'gentleman-like, comfortable house'; it has some fine rooms, including this one with panelling and a Jacobean-style plaster ceiling, all Victorian. I remember it being a Sunday afternoon treat in the 1950s to be taken here for tea by my grandfather, riding out from Gainsborough in his Ford V-8 Pilot. After tea my brother and I used to be sent out into the gardens to play, while the grown-ups lingered over their tea cups.

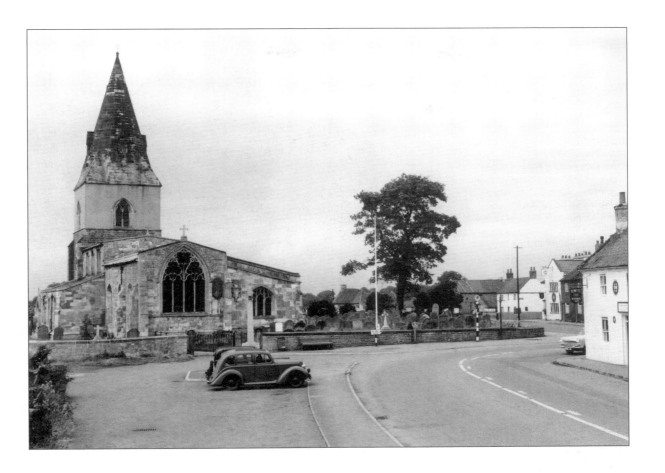

MISTERTON, *The Parish Church c1955* M235027

Moving on to the far north-east corner of the county, we reach
Misterton. It is situated in the drained fenland and carrs (copses) to the
west of the River Trent, through which meanders the River Idle on its
way to meet the river at West Stockwith. A long straggling village on a
(very) low ridge, Misterton has its medieval parish church at its north
end, with a fine stained glass window by John Piper in the Lady Chapel
added in 1965. The house with the butcher's shop on the right was
demolished in the 1960s for road improvement.

► **MISTERTON**
High Street c1955 M235024

East and south of the church, the High Street has a number of good houses, including the 18th-century Elm Farmhouse in the distance. Behind the cottages on the left towers the gable of the Methodist church, a grandiose building of 1878 where my great-grandfather was a lay preacher and leading light in the village's thriving Primitive Methodist church. To the left, out of view, is the former Temperance Hall of 1872.

◀ **MISTERTON**
Station Street c1955
M235025

Station Street turns east from the High Street, and once led to the railway station on the branch line from Gainsborough to Doncaster, closed since the 1960s. At the junction is the tower of the former Board Schools, built in 1872; the building to its right was demolished in the 1960s for junction improvements. My great-grandfather had his printing business at Station Villa in Station Road. Here he published *Durdey's Almanack* from 1878 until about 1916 – it was similar to Whitaker's, but more local.

▶ **MISTERTON**
The Canal Lock
c1955   M235048

The Chesterfield Canal passes south of the village, and this view looks from the 1930s road bridge on the A161, which by-passed the old winding lane of Station Street. This is the last lock on the canal before it reaches West Stockwith basin. The houses and cottages remain; the one to the left with the pantile roof and chimney is now a garden store to a more modern house, No 88. However, the Packet Inn (centre) has been demolished recently (2003), and the old brick bridge was rebuilt in the 1970s.

◀ **MISTERTON**
The View from the Old Bridge
c1955   M235017

From the old Station Street canal bridge, Frith's photographer looks past the Packet Inn, now utterly gone, towards the railway bridge, which still carries freight trains. However, Misterton station closed to passengers in the 1960s. The Chesterfield Canal opened in 1777, but by 1900 it was in serious decline, and it fell into disuse soon after this view was taken. In 1961 enthusiasts formed the Chesterfield Canal Society, and the section through Nottinghamshire is now largely restored.

▲ **MISTERTON,** *Pump Houses on the River Idle, Soss Lane c1955* M235019

At the end of Soss Lane, beyond the railway line, are two former pump houses with tall chimneys; their steam-powered beam engines are situated on the Mother Drain which runs parallel to the River Idle to join the River Trent near West Stockwith. The Mother Drain is part of the drainage system for the carrs or fens west of Misterton, and one of the pump houses is dated 1828. Long derelict, they have recently been restored and converted into dwellings - one is named The Pump House. This view looks west along the River Idle.

◄ **WEST STOCKWITH**
The Canal Lock c1965
W590005

The Chesterfield Canal, the Mother Drain and the River Idle all reach the River Trent at West Stockwith - the canal is the most southerly of the three. West Stockwith was already a river port, and the Chesterfield Canal greatly boosted the village's trade when the canal and its basin were opened in 1777. The lock in the foreground opens into the River Trent, which is behind the photographer; in the distance is Basin Bridge, with the still thriving Waterfront Inn to its right.

▶ **WEST STOCKWITH**
The Canal Basin
c1955 W590056

Frith's photographer was looking from the front of the Waterfront Inn towards the Trent lock, with the old lock keeper's cottage to its left and the warehouse to its right. The building at the far right now houses the West Stockwith Yacht Club, and was extended in the 1970s.

◀ **WEST STOCKWITH**
The Canal Basin c1955
W590020

To the left is the old warehouse, built in local red brick with a pantiled roof; its datestone in the gable facing the River Trent is inscribed 'November 1789'. The white-painted hipped-roofed building behind the cabin cruiser is another view of what is now the Yacht Club, much altered now, partly rebuilt and with single-storey extensions. The basin is nowadays filled with leisure craft and gaily painted narrow boats.

▲ **HARWORTH,** *The Game Cock, Bawtry Road c1955* H482010

An entire colliery village was laid out east of the Tickhill to Blyth road after 1922, and named Bircotes. Between this and the old village of Harworth more estates were built from the 1950s onwards. In this view on Bawtry Road we see the Game Cock pub, built in yellow brick in the mid 1950s and now an hotel. Beyond is the recreation ground, then surrounded by council houses.

◄ **HARWORTH**
All Saints' Church c1955
H482015

Moving west to the county's boundary with Yorkshire, our tour reaches Harworth, an old greatly expanded village lying east of the Tickhill to Blyth road. This is coal mining country, and despite all the 1980s and 1990s pit closures and the grassed-over slag heaps that dot west Nottinghamshire, Harworth still has its colliery. Around All Saints' parish church are a few older houses, but the church itself, apart from the medieval tower, was largely rebuilt in the 1860s.

► **OLDCOTES**
Main Street c1965   O141065

Still close to the Yorkshire county boundary and south-west of Harworth, Oldcotes village is situated at the crossroads of the A634 and A60; Main Street runs east from the A60 Doncaster Road south of the Blyth Road. The house on the left, South Royd, with its attached barn, has now had the paint removed from the stonework. A stream runs along the right-hand side of the road, and at the end and out of sight is St Helen's Roman Catholic church of about 1870, and rather good.

◄ **LANGOLD**
Doncaster Road Shopping Centre c1955 L349012

Continuing south towards Worksop on the A60, the route reaches Langold, situated a mile south of Oldcotes. The village was built to house the coalminers of nearby Costhorpe Colliery, now closed. Out of view on the left is the village, mostly neat former 1950s Coal Board and council houses, and on the right is the main shopping parade along the Doncaster Road. The village had its own cinema, the Palace, the white building with the semi-circular pediment; it is now a bar and snooker hall.

▶ **LANGOLD**
The Lake c1955
L349010

Immediately south-west of the village and approached via Church Street is Langold Country Park, dominated by a fine lake. It was laid out as the landscaped park to a country house that was never built, although the foundations were laid in 1818. Acquired by the Coal Board, the park was managed as a recreational facility for their mining village of Langold.

◀ **LANGOLD**
The Children's Swimming Pool c1955 L349017

When the Coal Board closed the mine, the park was taken over by Worksop Rural District Council; in 1974 it passed to the new Bassetlaw District Council, who now administer it. To the south of the lake the Coal Board built a children's swimming pool. It was later made rectangular, but now appears disused and empty of water. The buildings have been demolished, but the park is well used and the lake is popular with fishermen.

▲ **CARLTON IN LINDRICK,** *The Church Tower, the West Door c1960* C491004

Two miles south of Langold, Carlton in Lindrick is a village of two parts, the original village to the south and a large former colliery village with hard red brick semi-detached houses. At the heart of the old village to the west of the Doncaster Road is the parish church with its fine Anglo-Saxon west tower. This view is of the Norman west door in the tower, which was moved from the nave in 1831.

◄ **CARLTON IN LINDRICK**
The Mill House c1965
C491014

South of the church is Carlton Mill, an early 19th-century stone-built former watermill; the stream that powered it passes under the bridge to the right. The boulder to the right has been replaced by mill-stones, and the mill retains its cast iron 19th-century waterwheel. Beyond is the mid 19th-century The Lodge, rendered and picturesque. The drive it guarded led to the Georgian Carlton Hall, which was demolished in 1955; the family moved to nearby Wigthorpe.

CARLTON IN LINDRICK
High Road c1965 C491012

The main village had migrated east to the main through road before the colliery village was added. This view looks north along the Doncaster Road, with 1890s and 1920s semi-detached houses and villas to the left behind the foreground hedges. To the right, the large rendered building is the Methodist schoolroom, with the gable of the 1861 Methodist church beyond. The hipped-roofed building to the left is a former coaching inn, now partly a fish and chip shop.

CARLTON IN LINDRICK, *Wigthorpe c1965* C491017

Just south of Carlton is the hamlet of Wigthorpe, no more than a few stone houses and cottages on a tranquil lane now by-passed by the Doncaster Road. The distant building with the bay window is Wigthorpe Hall, late 18th-century and also in stone.

INDEX

Frith Book Co Titles

www.francisfrith.co.uk

The Frith Book Company publishes over 100 new titles each year. A selection of those currently available is listed below. For latest catalogue please contact Frith Book Co.
Town Books 96 pages, approximately 100 photos. **County and Themed Books** 128 pages, approximately 150 photos (unless specified). All titles hardback with laminated case and jacket, except those indicated pb (paperback)

Amersham, Chesham & Rickmansworth (pb)	1-85937-340-2	£9.99	Devon (pb)	1-85937-297-x	£9.99
Andover (pb)	1-85937-292-9	£9.99	Devon Churches (pb)	1-85937-250-3	£9.99
Aylesbury (pb)	1-85937-227-9	£9.99	Dorchester (pb)	1-85937-307-0	£9.99
Barnstaple (pb)	1-85937-300-3	£9.99	Dorset (pb)	1-85937-269-4	£9.99
Basildon Living Memories (pb)	1-85937-515-4	£9.99	Dorset Coast (pb)	1-85937-299-6	£9.99
Bath (pb)	1-85937-419-0	£9.99	Dorset Living Memories (pb)	1-85937-584-7	£9.99
Bedford (pb)	1-85937-205-8	£9.99	Down the Severn (pb)	1-85937-560-x	£9.99
Bedfordshire Living Memories	1-85937-513-8	£14.99	Down The Thames (pb)	1-85937-278-3	£9.99
Belfast (pb)	1-85937-303-8	£9.99	Down the Trent	1-85937-311-9	£14.99
Berkshire (pb)	1-85937-191-4	£9.99	East Anglia (pb)	1-85937-265-1	£9.99
Berkshire Churches	1-85937-170-1	£17.99	East Grinstead (pb)	1-85937-138-3	£9.99
Berkshire Living Memories	1-85937-332-1	£14.99	East London	1-85937-080-2	£14.99
Black Country	1-85937-497-2	£12.99	East Sussex (pb)	1-85937-606-1	£9.99
Blackpool (pb)	1-85937-393-3	£9.99	Eastbourne (pb)	1-85937-399-2	£9.99
Bognor Regis (pb)	1-85937-431-x	£9.99	Edinburgh (pb)	1-85937-193-0	£8.99
Bournemouth (pb)	1-85937-545-6	£9.99	England In The 1880s	1-85937-331-3	£17.99
Bradford (pb)	1-85937-204-x	£9.99	Essex - Second Selection	1-85937-456-5	£14.99
Bridgend (pb)	1-85937-386-0	£7.99	Essex (pb)	1-85937-270-8	£9.99
Bridgwater (pb)	1-85937-305-4	£9.99	Essex Coast	1-85937-342-9	£14.99
Bridport (pb)	1-85937-327-5	£9.99	Essex Living Memories	1-85937-490-5	£14.99
Brighton (pb)	1-85937-192-2	£8.99	Exeter	1-85937-539-1	£9.99
Bristol (pb)	1-85937-264-3	£9.99	Exmoor (pb)	1-85937-608-8	£9.99
British Life A Century Ago (pb)	1-85937-213-9	£9.99	Falmouth (pb)	1-85937-594-4	£9.99
Buckinghamshire (pb)	1-85937-200-7	£9.99	Folkestone (pb)	1-85937-124-8	£9.99
Camberley (pb)	1-85937-222-8	£9.99	Frome (pb)	1-85937-317-8	£9.99
Cambridge (pb)	1-85937-422-0	£9.99	Glamorgan	1-85937-488-3	£14.99
Cambridgeshire (pb)	1-85937-420-4	£9.99	Glasgow (pb)	1-85937-190-6	£9.99
Cambridgeshire Villages	1-85937-523-5	£14.99	Glastonbury (pb)	1-85937-338-0	£7.99
Canals And Waterways (pb)	1-85937-291-0	£9.99	Gloucester (pb)	1-85937-232-5	£9.99
Canterbury Cathedral (pb)	1-85937-179-5	£9.99	Gloucestershire (pb)	1-85937-561-8	£9.99
Cardiff (pb)	1-85937-093-4	£9.99	Great Yarmouth (pb)	1-85937-426-3	£9.99
Carmarthenshire (pb)	1-85937-604-5	£9.99	Greater Manchester (pb)	1-85937-266-x	£9.99
Chelmsford (pb)	1-85937-310-0	£9.99	Guildford (pb)	1-85937-410-7	£9.99
Cheltenham (pb)	1-85937-095-0	£9.99	Hampshire (pb)	1-85937-279-1	£9.99
Cheshire (pb)	1-85937-271-6	£9.99	Harrogate (pb)	1-85937-423-9	£9.99
Chester (pb)	1-85937-382 8	£9.99	Hastings and Bexhill (pb)	1-85937-131-0	£9.99
Chesterfield (pb)	1-85937-378-x	£9.99	Heart of Lancashire (pb)	1-85937-197-3	£9.99
Chichester (pb)	1-85937-228-7	£9.99	Helston (pb)	1-85937-214-7	£9.99
Churches of East Cornwall (pb)	1-85937-249-x	£9.99	Hereford (pb)	1-85937-175-2	£9.99
Churches of Hampshire (pb)	1-85937-207-4	£9.99	Herefordshire (pb)	1-85937-567-7	£9.99
Cinque Ports & Two Ancient Towns	1-85937-492-1	£14.99	Herefordshire Living Memories	1-85937-514-6	£14.99
Colchester (pb)	1-85937-188-4	£8.99	Hertfordshire (pb)	1-85937-247-3	£9.99
Cornwall (pb)	1-85937-229-5	£9.99	Horsham (pb)	1-85937-432-8	£9.99
Cornwall Living Memories	1-85937-248-1	£14.99	Humberside (pb)	1-85937-605-3	£9.99
Cotswolds (pb)	1-85937-230-9	£9.99	Hythe, Romney Marsh, Ashford (pb)	1-85937-256-2	£9.99
Cotswolds Living Memories	1-85937-255-4	£14.99	Ipswich (pb)	1-85937-424-7	£9.99
County Durham (pb)	1-85937-398-4	£9.99	Isle of Man (pb)	1-85937-268-6	£9.99
Croydon Living Memories (pb)	1-85937-162-0	£9.99	Isle of Wight (pb)	1-85937-429-8	£9.99
Cumbria (pb)	1-85937-621-5	£9.99	Isle of Wight Living Memories	1-85937-304-6	£14.99
Derby (pb)	1-85937-367-4	£9.99	Kent (pb)	1-85937-189-2	£9.99
Derbyshire (pb)	1-85937-196-5	£9.99	Kent Living Memories(pb)	1-85937-401-8	£9.99
Derbyshire Living Memories	1-85937-330-5	£14.99	Kings Lynn (pb)	1-85937-334-8	£9.99

Available from your local bookshop or from the publisher

Frith Book Co Titles (continued)

Title	ISBN	Price	Title	ISBN	Price
Lake District (pb)	1-85937-275-9	£9.99	Sherborne (pb)	1-85937-301-1	£9.99
Lancashire Living Memories	1-85937-335-6	£14.99	Shrewsbury (pb)	1-85937-325-9	£9.99
Lancaster, Morecambe, Heysham (pb)	1-85937-233-3	£9.99	Shropshire (pb)	1-85937-326-7	£9.99
Leeds (pb)	1-85937-202-3	£9.99	Shropshire Living Memories	1-85937-643-6	£14.99
Leicester (pb)	1-85937-381-x	£9.99	Somerset	1-85937-153-1	£14.99
Leicestershire & Rutland Living Memories	1-85937-500-6	£12.99	South Devon Coast	1-85937-107-8	£14.99
Leicestershire (pb)	1-85937-185-x	£9.99	South Devon Living Memories (pb)	1-85937-609-6	£9.99
Lighthouses	1-85937-257-0	£9.99	South East London (pb)	1-85937-263-5	£9.99
Lincoln (pb)	1-85937-380-1	£9.99	South Somerset	1-85937-318-6	£14.99
Lincolnshire (pb)	1-85937-433-6	£9.99	South Wales	1-85937-519-7	£14.99
Liverpool and Merseyside (pb)	1-85937-234-1	£9.99	Southampton (pb)	1-85937-427-1	£9.99
London (pb)	1-85937-183-3	£9.99	Southend (pb)	1-85937-313-5	£9.99
London Living Memories	1-85937-454-9	£14.99	Southport (pb)	1-85937-425-5	£9.99
Ludlow (pb)	1-85937-176-0	£9.99	St Albans (pb)	1-85937-341-0	£9.99
Luton (pb)	1-85937-235-x	£9.99	St Ives (pb)	1-85937-415-8	£9.99
Maidenhead (pb)	1-85937-339-9	£9.99	Stafford Living Memories (pb)	1-85937-503-0	£9.99
Maidstone (pb)	1-85937-391-7	£9.99	Staffordshire (pb)	1-85937-308-9	£9.99
Manchester (pb)	1-85937-198-1	£9.99	Stourbridge (pb)	1-85937-530-8	£9.99
Marlborough (pb)	1-85937-336-4	£9.99	Stratford upon Avon (pb)	1-85937-388-7	£9.99
Middlesex	1-85937-158-2	£14.99	Suffolk (pb)	1-85937-221-x	£9.99
Monmouthshire	1-85937-532-4	£14.99	Suffolk Coast (pb)	1-85937-610-x	£9.99
New Forest (pb)	1-85937-390-9	£9.99	Surrey (pb)	1-85937-240-6	£9.99
Newark (pb)	1-85937-366-6	£9.99	Surrey Living Memories	1-85937-328-3	£14.99
Newport, Wales (pb)	1-85937-258-9	£9.99	Sussex (pb)	1-85937-184-1	£9.99
Newquay (pb)	1-85937-421-2	£9.99	Sutton (pb)	1-85937-337-2	£9.99
Norfolk (pb)	1-85937-195-7	£9.99	Swansea (pb)	1-85937-167-1	£9.99
Norfolk Broads	1-85937-486-7	£14.99	Taunton (pb)	1-85937-314-3	£9.99
Norfolk Living Memories (pb)	1-85937-402-6	£9.99	Tees Valley & Cleveland (pb)	1-85937-623-1	£9.99
North Buckinghamshire	1-85937-626-6	£14.99	Teignmouth (pb)	1-85937-370-4	£7.99
North Devon Living Memories	1-85937-261-9	£14.99	Thanet (pb)	1-85937-116-7	£9.99
North Hertfordshire	1-85937-547-2	£14.99	Tiverton (pb)	1-85937-178-7	£9.99
North London (pb)	1-85937-403-4	£9.99	Torbay (pb)	1-85937-597-9	£9.99
North Somerset	1-85937-302-x	£14.99	Truro (pb)	1-85937-598-7	£9.99
North Wales (pb)	1-85937-298-8	£9.99	Victorian & Edwardian Dorset	1-85937-254-6	£14.99
North Yorkshire (pb)	1-85937-236-8	£9.99	Victorian & Edwardian Kent (pb)	1-85937-624-X	£9.99
Northamptonshire Living Memories	1-85937-529-4	£14.99	Victorian & Edwardian Maritime Album (pb)	1-85937-622-3	£9.99
Northamptonshire	1-85937-150-7	£14.99	Victorian and Edwardian Sussex (pb)	1-85937-625-8	£9.99
Northumberland Tyne & Wear (pb)	1-85937-281-3	£9.99	Villages of Devon (pb)	1-85937-293-7	£9.99
Northumberland	1-85937-522-7	£14.99	Villages of Kent (pb)	1-85937-294-5	£9.99
Norwich (pb)	1-85937-194-9	£8.99	Villages of Sussex (pb)	1-85937-295-3	£9.99
Nottingham (pb)	1-85937-324-0	£9.99	Warrington (pb)	1-85937-507-3	£9.99
Nottinghamshire (pb)	1-85937-187-6	£9.99	Warwick (pb)	1-85937-518-9	£9.99
Oxford (pb)	1-85937-411-5	£9.99	Warwickshire (pb)	1-85937-203-1	£9.99
Oxfordshire (pb)	1-85937-430-1	£9.99	Welsh Castles (pb)	1-85937-322-4	£9.99
Oxfordshire Living Memories	1-85937-525-1	£14.99	West Midlands (pb)	1-85937-289-9	£9.99
Paignton (pb)	1-85937-374-7	£7.99	West Sussex (pb)	1-85937-607-x	£9.99
Peak District (pb)	1-85937-280-5	£9.99	West Yorkshire (pb)	1-85937-201-5	£9.99
Pembrokeshire	1-85937-262-7	£14.99	Weston Super Mare (pb)	1-85937-306-2	£9.99
Penzance (pb)	1-85937-595-2	£9.99	Weymouth (pb)	1-85937-209-0	£9.99
Peterborough (pb)	1-85937-219-8	£9.99	Wiltshire (pb)	1-85937-277-5	£9.99
Picturesque Harbours	1-85937-208-2	£14.99	Wiltshire Churches (pb)	1-85937-171-x	£9.99
Piers	1-85937-237-6	£17.99	Wiltshire Living Memories (pb)	1-85937-396-8	£9.99
Plymouth (pb)	1-85937-389-5	£9.99	Winchester (pb)	1-85937-428-x	£9.99
Poole & Sandbanks (pb)	1-85937-251-1	£9.99	Windsor (pb)	1-85937-333-x	£9.99
Preston (pb)	1-85937-212-0	£9.99	Wokingham & Bracknell (pb)	1-85937-329-1	£9.99
Reading (pb)	1-85937-238-4	£9.99	Woodbridge (pb)	1-85937-498-0	£9.99
Redhill to Reigate (pb)	1-85937-596-0	£9.99	Worcester (pb)	1-85937-165-5	£9.99
Ringwood (pb)	1-85937-384-4	£7.99	Worcestershire Living Memories	1-85937-489-1	£14.99
Romford (pb)	1-85937-319-2	£9.99	Worcestershire	1-85937-152-3	£14.99
Royal Tunbridge Wells (pb)	1-85937-504-9	£9.99	York (pb)	1-85937-199-x	£9.99
Salisbury (pb)	1-85937-239-2	£9.99	Yorkshire (pb)	1-85937-186-8	£9.99
Scarborough (pb)	1-85937-379-8	£9.99	Yorkshire Coastal Memories	1-85937-506-5	£14.99
Sevenoaks and Tonbridge (pb)	1-85937-392-5	£9.99	Yorkshire Dales	1-85937-502-2	£14.99
Sheffield & South Yorks (pb)	1-85937-267-8	£9.99	Yorkshire Living Memories (pb)	1-85937-397-6	£9.99

See Frith books on the internet at www.francisfrith.co.uk

FRITH PRODUCTS & SERVICES

Francis Frith would doubtless be pleased to know that the pioneering publishing venture he started in 1860 still continues today. Over a hundred and forty years later, The Francis Frith Collection continues in the same innovative tradition and is now one of the foremost publishers of vintage photographs in the world. Some of the current activities include:

Interior Decoration

Today Frith's photographs can be seen framed and as giant wall murals in thousands of pubs, restaurants, hotels, banks, retail stores and other public buildings throughout the country. In every case they enhance the unique local atmosphere of the places they depict and provide reminders of gentler days in an increasingly busy and frenetic world.

Product Promotions

Frith products are used by many major companies to promote the sales of their own products or to reinforce their own history and heritage. Frith promotions have been used by Hovis bread, Courage beers, Scots Porage Oats, Colman's mustard, Cadbury's foods, Mellow Birds coffee, Dunhill pipe tobacco, Guinness, and Bulmer's Cider.

Genealogy and Family History

As the interest in family history and roots grows world-wide, more and more people are turning to Frith's photographs of Great Britain for images of the towns, villages and streets where their ancestors lived; and, of course, photographs of the churches and chapels where their ancestors were christened, married and buried are an essential part of every genealogy tree and family album.

Frith Products

All Frith photographs are available Framed or just as Mounted Prints and Posters (size 23 x 16 inches). These may be ordered from the address below. From time to time other products - Address Books, Calendars, Table Mats, etc - are available.

The Internet

Already fifty thousand Frith photographs can be viewed and purchased on the internet through the Frith websites and a myriad of partner sites.

For more detailed information on Frith companies and products, look at these sites:

www.francisfrith.co.uk
www.francisfrith.com
(for North American visitors)

See the complete list of Frith Books at:

www.francisfrith.co.uk

This web site is regularly updated with the latest list of publications from the Frith Book Company. If you wish to buy books relating to another part of the country that your local bookshop does not stock, you may purchase on-line.

For further information, trade, or author enquiries please contact us at the address below:
The Francis Frith Collection, Frith's Barn, Teffont, Salisbury, Wiltshire, England SP3 5QP.
Tel: +44 (0)1722 716 376 Fax: +44 (0)1722 716 881 Email: sales@francisfrith.co.uk

See Frith books on the internet at www.francisfrith.co.uk

FREE MOUNTED PRINT

Mounted Print
Overall size 14 x 11 inches

Fill in and cut out this voucher and return
it with your remittance for £2.25 (to cover postage and handling). Offer valid for delivery to UK addresses only.

Choose any photograph included in this book.
Your SEPIA print will be A4 in size. It will be mounted in a cream mount with a burgundy rule line (overall size 14 x 11 inches).

Order additional Mounted Prints
at HALF PRICE (only £7.49 each*)
If you would like to order more Frith prints from this book, possibly as gifts for friends and family, you can buy them at half price (with no additional postage and handling costs).

Have your Mounted Prints framed
For an extra £14.95 per print* you can have your mounted print(s) framed in an elegant polished wood and gilt moulding, overall size 16 x 13 inches (no additional postage and handling required).

---

* IMPORTANT!

These special prices are only available if you order at the same time as you order your free mounted print. You must use the ORIGINAL VOUCHER on this page (no copies permitted). We can only despatch to one address.

Send completed Voucher form to:
The Francis Frith Collection, Frith's Barn, Teffont, Salisbury, Wiltshire SP3 5QP

CHOOSE ANY IMAGE FROM THIS BOOK

Voucher for *FREE* and Reduced Price Frith Prints

Please do not photocopy this voucher. Only the original is valid, so please fill it in, cut it out and return it to us with your order.

Picture ref no	Page no	Qty	Mounted @ £7.49	Framed + £14.95	Total Cost
		1	Free of charge*	£	£
			£7.49	£	£
			£7.49	£	£
			£7.49	£	£
			£7.49	£	£
			£7.49	£	£

Please allow 28 days for delivery	* Post & handling (UK)	£2.25
	Total Order Cost	£

Title of this book . . . .

I enclose a cheque/postal order for £ . . . .
made payable to 'The Francis Frith Collection'

OR please debit my Mastercard / Visa / Switch / Amex card
(credit cards please on all overseas orders), details below

Card Number

Issue No (Switch only)   Valid from (Amex/Switch)

Expires   Signature

Name Mr/Mrs/Ms ....

Address ....

....

....

.... Postcode ....

Daytime Tel No ....

Email ....

Valid to 31/12/05

Would you like to find out more about Francis Frith?

We have recently recruited some entertaining speakers who are happy to visit local groups, clubs and societies to give an illustrated talk documenting Frith's travels and photographs. If you are a member of such a group and are interested in hosting a presentation, we would love to hear from you.

Our speakers bring with them a small selection of our local town and county books, together with sample prints. They are happy to take orders. A small proportion of the order value is donated to the group who have hosted the presentation. The talks are therefore an excellent way of fundraising for small groups and societies.

Can you help us with information about any of the Frith photographs in this book?

We are gradually compiling an historical record for each of the photographs in the Frith archive. It is always fascinating to find out the names of the people shown in the pictures, as well as insights into the shops, buildings and other features depicted.

If you recognize anyone in the photographs in this book, or if you have information not already included in the author's caption, do let us know. We would love to hear from you, and will try to publish it in future books or articles.

Our production team

Frith books are produced by a small dedicated team at offices in the converted Grade II listed 18th-century barn at Teffont near Salisbury, illustrated above. Most have worked with the Frith Collection for many years. All have in common one quality: they have a passion for the Frith Collection. The team is constantly expanding, but currently includes:

Jason Buck, John Buck, Douglas Mitchell-Burns, Ruth Butler, Heather Crisp, Isobel Hall, Julian Hight, Peter Horne, James Kinnear, Karen Kinnear, Tina Leary, David Marsh, Sue Molloy, Kate Rotondetto, Dean Scource, Eliza Sackett, Terence Sackett, Sandra Sampson, Adrian Sanders, Sandra Sanger, Julia Skinner, Lewis Taylor, Shelley Tolcher and Lorraine Tuck.